TRANSFORMERS™

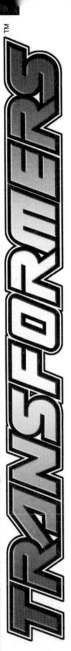

ASPECTS OF EVIL!

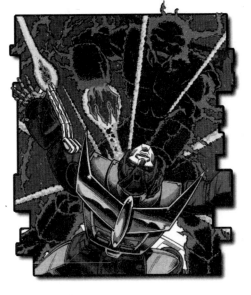

TRANSFORMERS™: ASPECTS OF EVIL!
ISBN 1 84576 055 7

Published by Titan Books,
a division of Titan Publishing Group Ltd.
144 Southwark St
London SE1 0UP
UK

HASBRO and its logo, TRANSFORMERS and all related characters are trademarks of Hasbro and are
used with permission. © 2005 Hasbro. All Rights Reserved. No portion of this book may be
reproduced or transmitted in any form or by any means, without the express written permission of
the publisher. Names, characters, places and incidents featured in this publication are either
the product of the author's imagination or used fictitiously. Any resemblance to actual persons
(living or dead) is entirely coincidental.

This book collects the black and white stories from *Transformers* #223-227, 251-254, 235-236,
240 & 245-247 originally published in single-issue form by Marvel Comics, UK.

A CIP catalogue record for this title is available from the British Library.

First paperback edition: May 2005
2 4 6 8 10 9 7 5 3 1

Printed in Italy.

Also available from Titan Books...

Transformers: All Fall Down (ISBN: 1 84023 300 1)
Transformers: End of the Road (ISBN: 1 84023 372 9)
Transformers: Primal Scream (ISBN: 1 84023 401 6)
Transformers: Matrix Quest (ISBN: 1 84023 471 7)
Transformers: Dark Designs (ISBN: 1 84023 525 X)
Transformers: Rage in Heaven (ISBN: 1 84023 528 4)
Transformers: Beginnings (ISBN: 1 84023 623 X)
Transformers: New Order (ISBN: 1 84023 624 8)
Transformers: Cybertron Redux (ISBN: 1 84023 657 4)
Transformers: Showdown (ISBN: 1 84023 681 7)
Transformers: Breakdown (ISBN: 1 84023 791 0)
Transformers: Treason (ISBN: 1 84023 844 5)
Transformers: Trial By Fire (ISBN: 184023 950 6)
Transformers: Maximum Force (ISBN: 1 84023 955 7)
Transformers: Dark Star (ISBN: 1 84023 960 3)
Transformers: Last Stand (ISBN: 1 84576 008 5)

Transformers: Target 2006 (ISBN: 1 84023 510 1)
Transformers: Fallen Angel (ISBN: 1 84023 511 X)
Transformers: Legacy of Unicron (ISBN: 1 84023 578 0)
Transformers: Space Pirates (ISBN: 1 84023 619 1)
Transformers: Time Wars (ISBN 1 84023 647 7)
Transformers: City of Fear (ISBN 1 84023 671 X)
Transformers: Dinobot Hunt (ISBN 1 84023 789 9)
Transformers: Prey (ISBN: 1 84023 831 3)
Transformers: Second Generation (ISBN: 1 84023 935 2)

What did you think of this book? We love to hear from our readers.
Please email us at: readerfeedback@titanemail.com or write to us at the above address.
You can also visit us at www.titanbooks.com

Cover art by Stephen Baskerville

NIAGARA FALLS PUBLIC LIBRARY

TRANSFORMERS™

ASPECTS OF EVIL!

Furman
Wildman
Johnson

Titan Books

TRANSFORMERS™

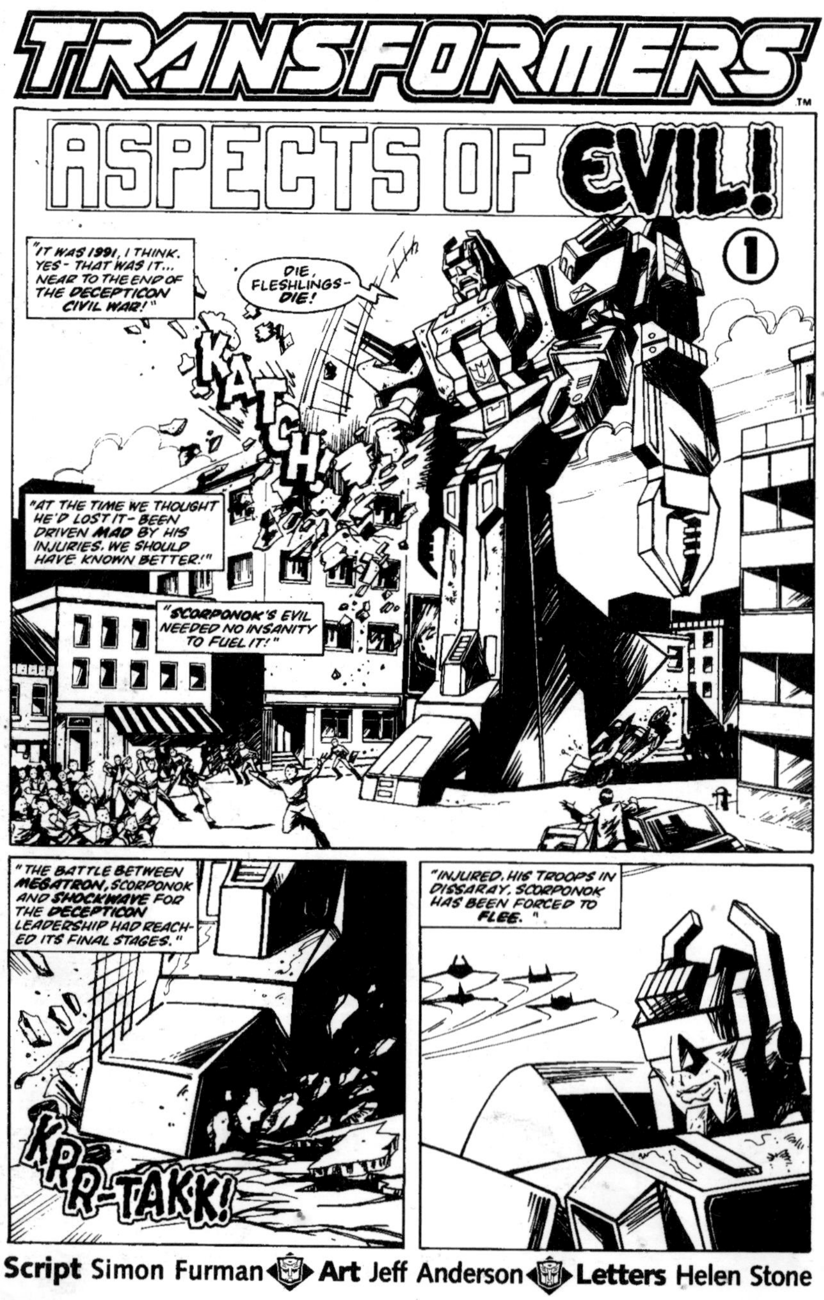
ASPECTS OF EVIL!
1
"IT WAS 1991, I THINK. YES - THAT WAS IT... NEAR TO THE END OF THE DECEPTICON CIVIL WAR!"
DIE, FLESHLINGS- DIE!
KATCH!
"AT THE TIME WE THOUGHT HE'D LOST IT - BEEN DRIVEN MAD BY HIS INJURIES. WE SHOULD HAVE KNOWN BETTER!"
"SCORPONOK'S EVIL NEEDED NO INSANITY TO FUEL IT!"
"THE BATTLE BETWEEN MEGATRON, SCORPONOK AND SHOCKWAVE FOR THE DECEPTICON LEADERSHIP HAD REACHED ITS FINAL STAGES."
KRR-TAKK!
"INJURED, HIS TROOPS IN DISSARAY, SCORPONOK HAS BEEN FORCED TO FLEE."

Script Simon Furman **Art** Jeff Anderson **Letters** Helen Stone

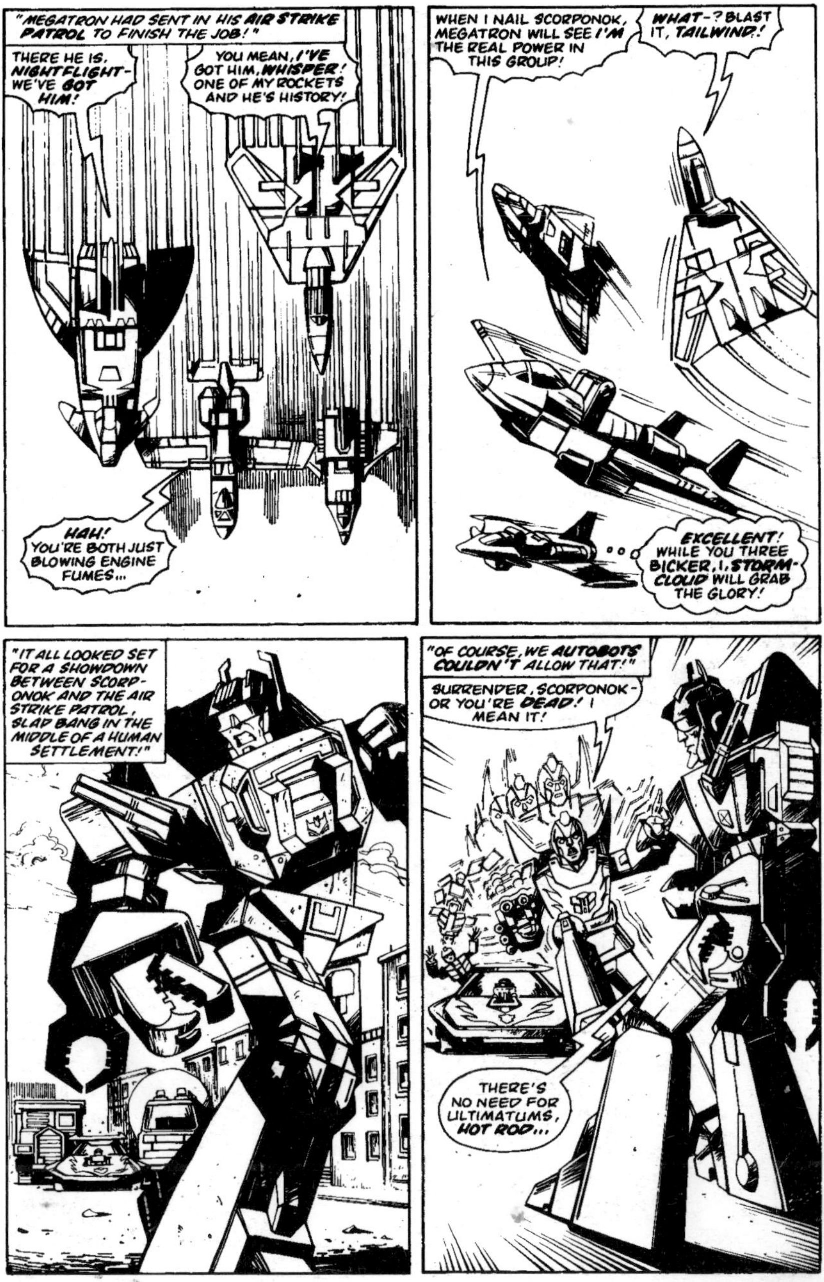
"MEGATRON HAD SENT IN HIS AIR STRIKE PATROL TO FINISH THE JOB!"
THERE HE IS, NIGHTFLIGHT- WE'VE GOT HIM!
YOU MEAN, I'VE GOT HIM, WHISPER! ONE OF MY ROCKETS AND HE'S HISTORY!
HAH! YOU'RE BOTH JUST BLOWING ENGINE FUMES...
WHEN I NAIL SCORPONOK, MEGATRON WILL SEE I'M THE REAL POWER IN THIS GROUP!
WHAT-? BLAST IT, TAILWIND!
EXCELLENT! WHILE YOU THREE BICKER, I, STORMCLOUD WILL GRAB THE GLORY!
"IT ALL LOOKED SET FOR A SHOWDOWN BETWEEN SCORPONOK AND THE AIR STRIKE PATROL, SLAP BANG IN THE MIDDLE OF A HUMAN SETTLEMENT!"
"OF COURSE, WE AUTOBOTS COULDN'T ALLOW THAT!"
SURRENDER, SCORPONOK - OR YOU'RE DEAD! I MEAN IT!
THERE'S NO NEED FOR ULTIMATUMS, HOT ROD...

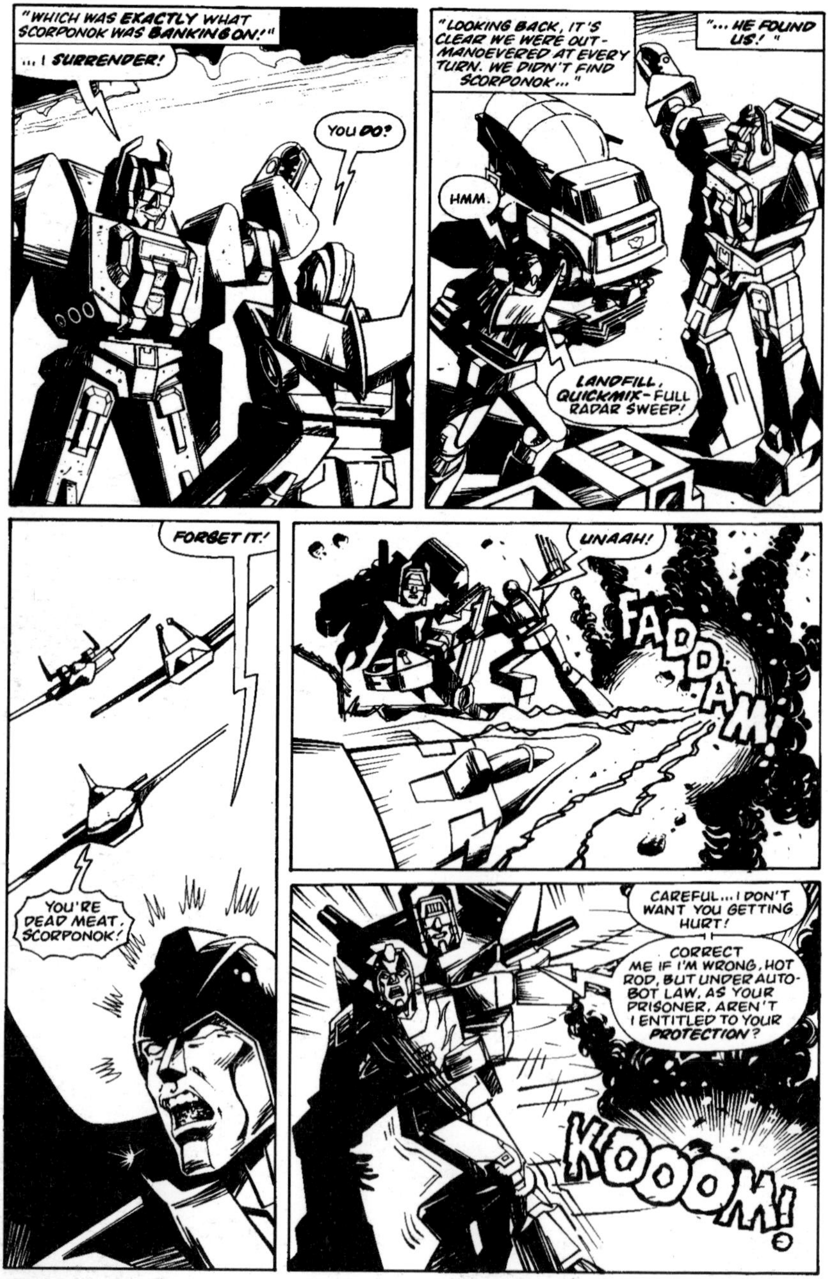
"WHICH WAS EXACTLY WHAT SCORPONOK WAS BANKING ON!"
...I SURRENDER!
YOU DO?
"LOOKING BACK, IT'S CLEAR WE WERE OUT-MANOEVERED AT EVERY TURN. WE DIDN'T FIND SCORPONOK..."
"...HE FOUND US!"
HMM.
LANDFILL, QUICKMIX- FULL RADAR SWEEP!
FORGET IT!
YOU'RE DEAD MEAT, SCORPONOK!
UNAAH!
FADDAM!
CAREFUL...I DON'T WANT YOU GETTING HURT!
CORRECT ME IF I'M WRONG, HOT ROD, BUT UNDER AUTO-BOT LAW, AS YOUR PRISONER, AREN'T I ENTITLED TO YOUR PROTECTION?
KOOOOM!

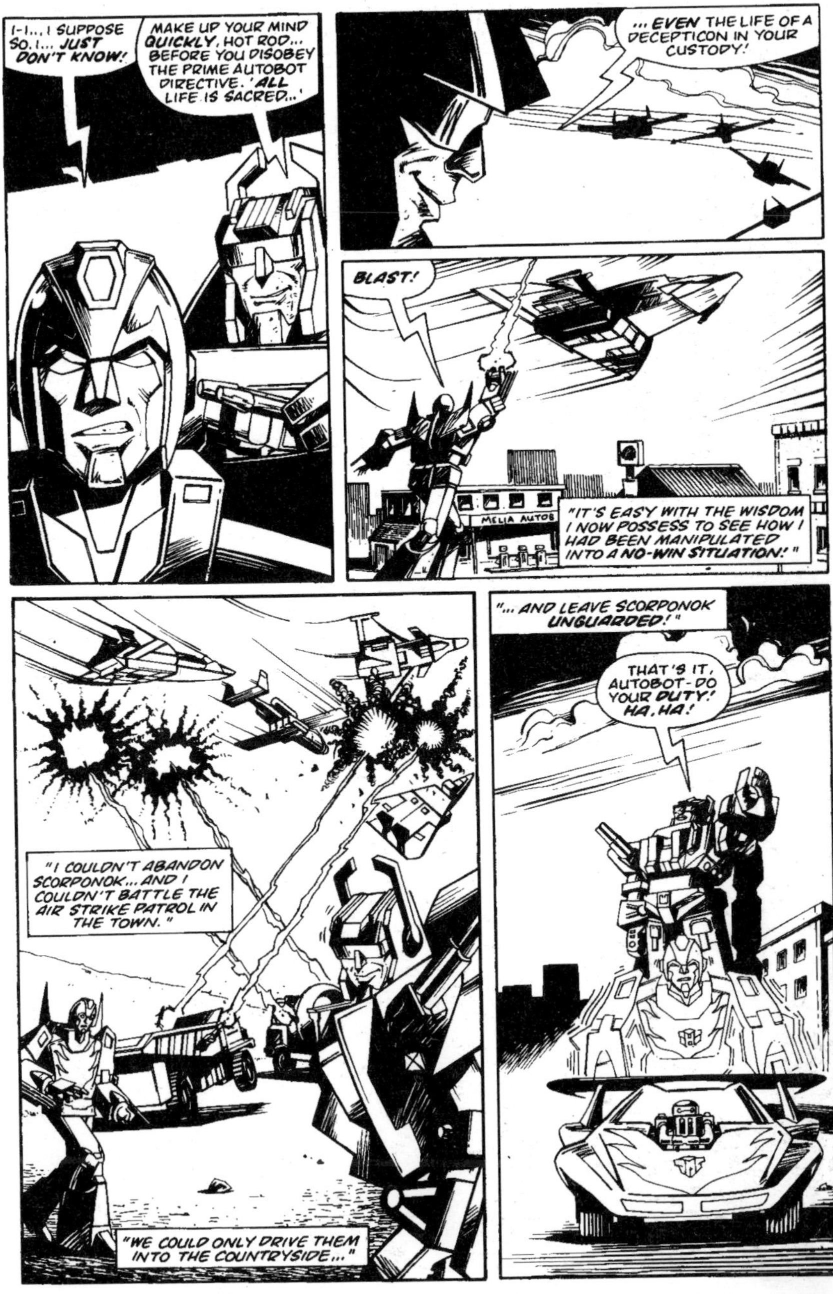
I-I... I SUPPOSE SO. I... JUST DON'T KNOW!
MAKE UP YOUR MIND QUICKLY, HOT ROD... BEFORE YOU DISOBEY THE PRIME AUTOBOT DIRECTIVE. 'ALL LIFE IS SACRED...'
...EVEN THE LIFE OF A DECEPTICON IN YOUR CUSTODY!
BLAST!
MELIA AUTOS
"IT'S EASY WITH THE WISDOM I NOW POSSESS TO SEE HOW I HAD BEEN MANIPULATED INTO A NO-WIN SITUATION!"
"I COULDN'T ABANDON SCORPONOK... AND I COULDN'T BATTLE THE AIR STRIKE PATROL IN THE TOWN."
"WE COULD ONLY DRIVE THEM INTO THE COUNTRYSIDE..."
"...AND LEAVE SCORPONOK UNGUARDED!"
THAT'S IT, AUTOBOT - DO YOUR DUTY! HA, HA!

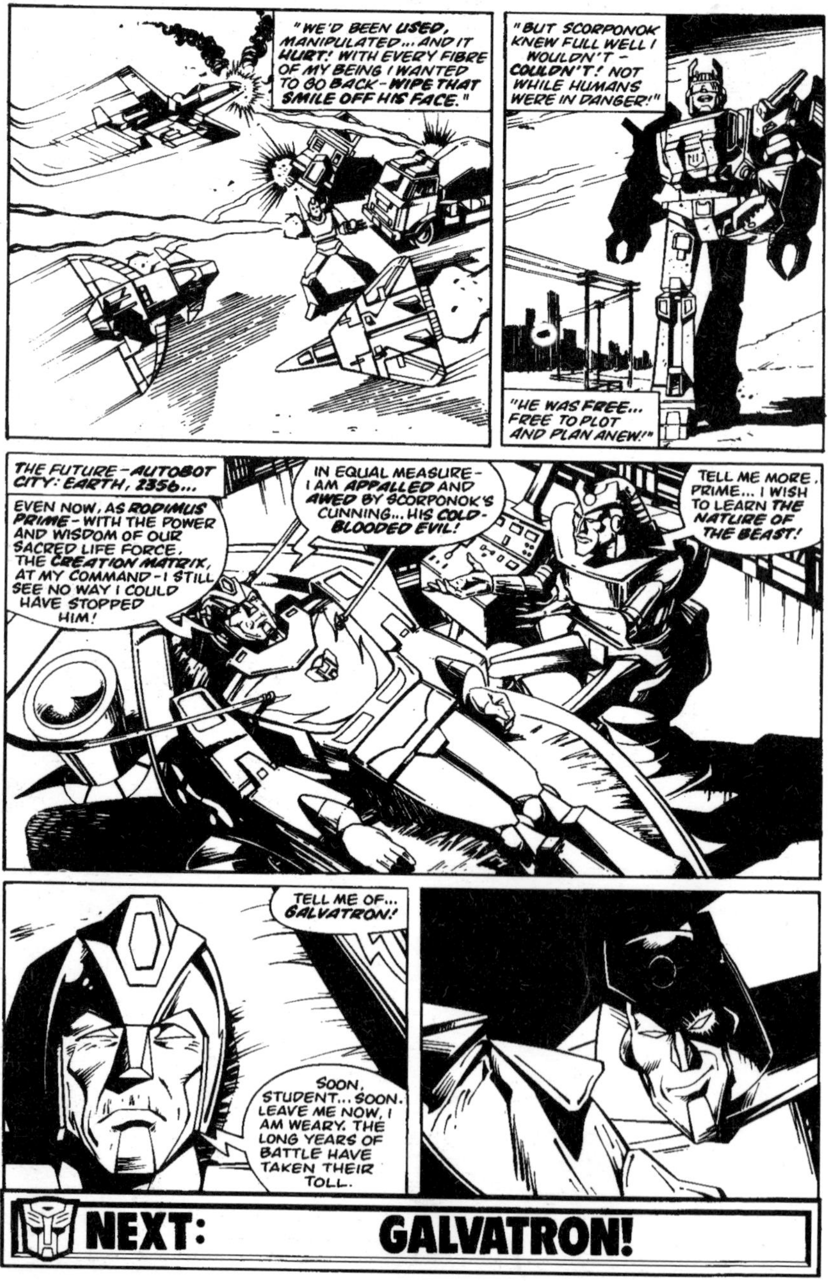
"WE'D BEEN USED, MANIPULATED... AND IT HURT! WITH EVERY FIBRE OF MY BEING I WANTED TO GO BACK - WIPE THAT SMILE OFF HIS FACE."
"BUT SCORPONOK KNEW FULL WELL I WOULDN'T - COULDN'T! NOT WHILE HUMANS WERE IN DANGER!"
"HE WAS FREE... FREE TO PLOT AND PLAN ANEW!"
THE FUTURE - AUTOBOT CITY: EARTH, 2356...
EVEN NOW, AS RODIMUS PRIME - WITH THE POWER AND WISDOM OF OUR SACRED LIFE FORCE, THE CREATION MATRIX, AT MY COMMAND - I STILL SEE NO WAY I COULD HAVE STOPPED HIM!
IN EQUAL MEASURE - I AM APPALLED AND AWED BY SCORPONOK'S CUNNING... HIS COLD-BLOODED EVIL!
TELL ME MORE, PRIME... I WISH TO LEARN THE NATURE OF THE BEAST!
TELL ME OF... GALVATRON!
SOON, STUDENT... SOON. LEAVE ME NOW, I AM WEARY. THE LONG YEARS OF BATTLE HAVE TAKEN THEIR TOLL.

NEXT: GALVATRON!

TRANSFORMERS™

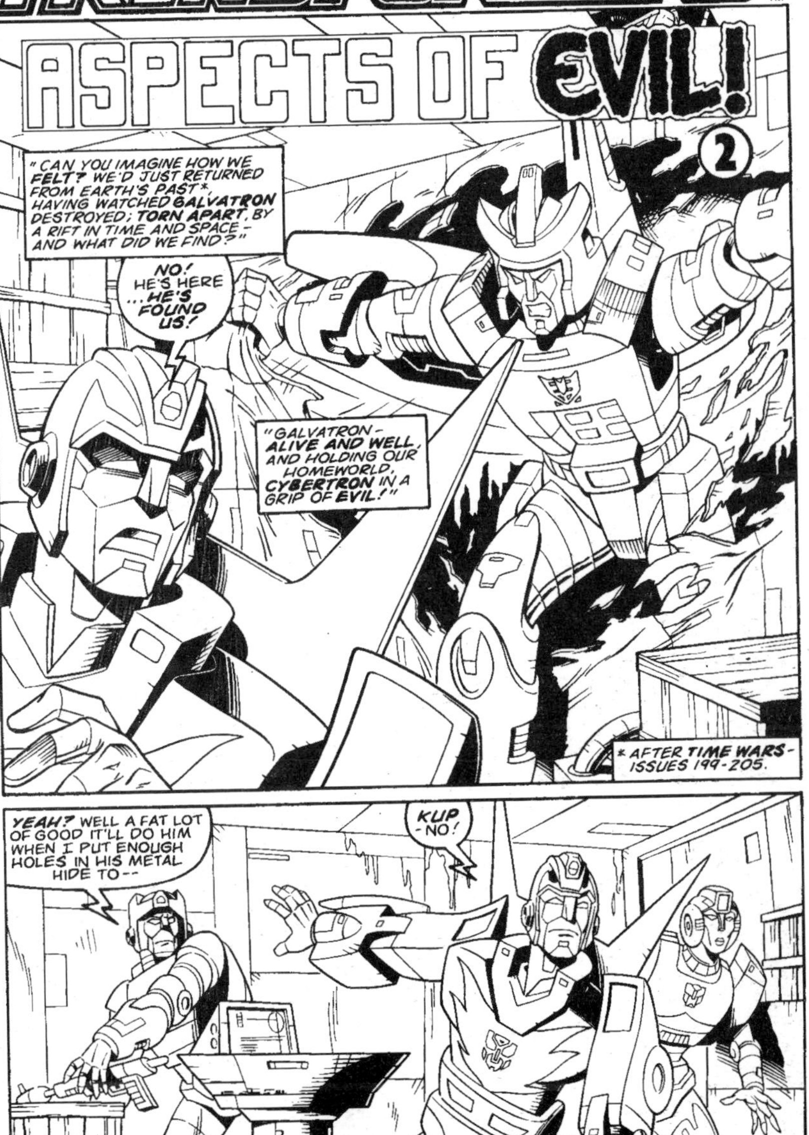
ASPECTS OF EVIL! 2
"CAN YOU IMAGINE HOW WE FELT? WE'D JUST RETURNED FROM EARTH'S PAST*, HAVING WATCHED GALVATRON DESTROYED; TORN APART, BY A RIFT IN TIME AND SPACE – AND WHAT DID WE FIND?"
NO! HE'S HERE ...HE'S FOUND US!
"GALVATRON – ALIVE AND WELL, AND HOLDING OUR HOMEWORLD, CYBERTRON IN A GRIP OF EVIL!"
* AFTER TIME WARS – ISSUES 199-205.
YEAH? WELL A FAT LOT OF GOOD IT'LL DO HIM WHEN I PUT ENOUGH HOLES IN HIS METAL HIDE TO--
KUP – NO!

Script Simon Furman · **Pencils** Art Wetherell · **Inks** Simon Coleby · **Letters** Glib

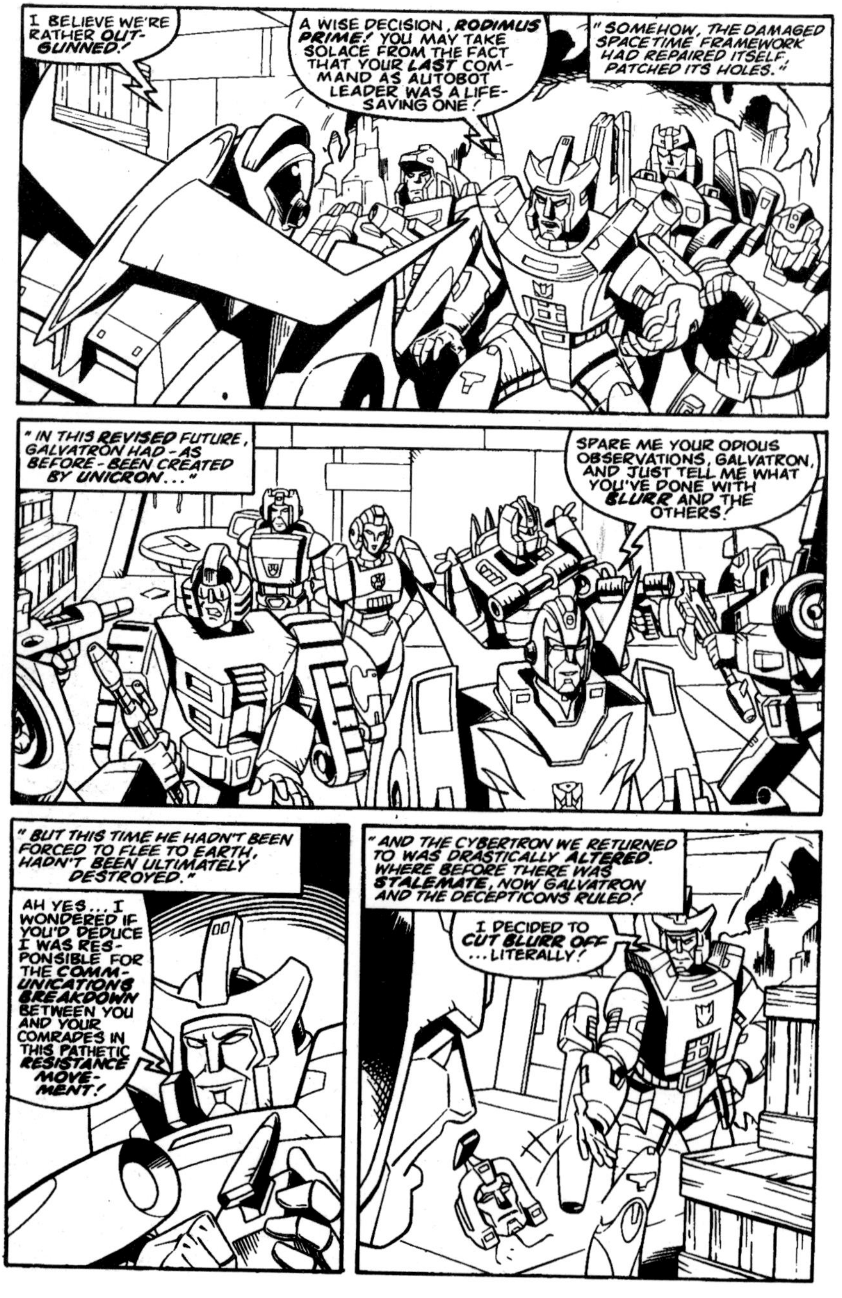
I BELIEVE WE'RE RATHER OUT-GUNNED!
A WISE DECISION, RODIMUS PRIME! YOU MAY TAKE SOLACE FROM THE FACT THAT YOUR LAST COMMAND AS AUTOBOT LEADER WAS A LIFE-SAVING ONE!
"SOMEHOW, THE DAMAGED SPACETIME FRAMEWORK HAD REPAIRED ITSELF, PATCHED ITS HOLES."
"IN THIS REVISED FUTURE, GALVATRON HAD - AS BEFORE - BEEN CREATED BY UNICRON..."
SPARE ME YOUR ODIOUS OBSERVATIONS, GALVATRON, AND JUST TELL ME WHAT YOU'VE DONE WITH BLURR AND THE OTHERS!
"BUT THIS TIME HE HADN'T BEEN FORCED TO FLEE TO EARTH, HADN'T BEEN ULTIMATELY DESTROYED."
AH YES... I WONDERED IF YOU'D DEDUCE I WAS RESPONSIBLE FOR THE COMMUNICATIONS BREAKDOWN BETWEEN YOU AND YOUR COMRADES IN THIS PATHETIC RESISTANCE MOVEMENT!
"AND THE CYBERTRON WE RETURNED TO WAS DRASTICALLY ALTERED. WHERE BEFORE THERE WAS STALEMATE, NOW GALVATRON AND THE DECEPTICONS RULED!"
I DECIDED TO CUT BLURR OFF ...LITERALLY!

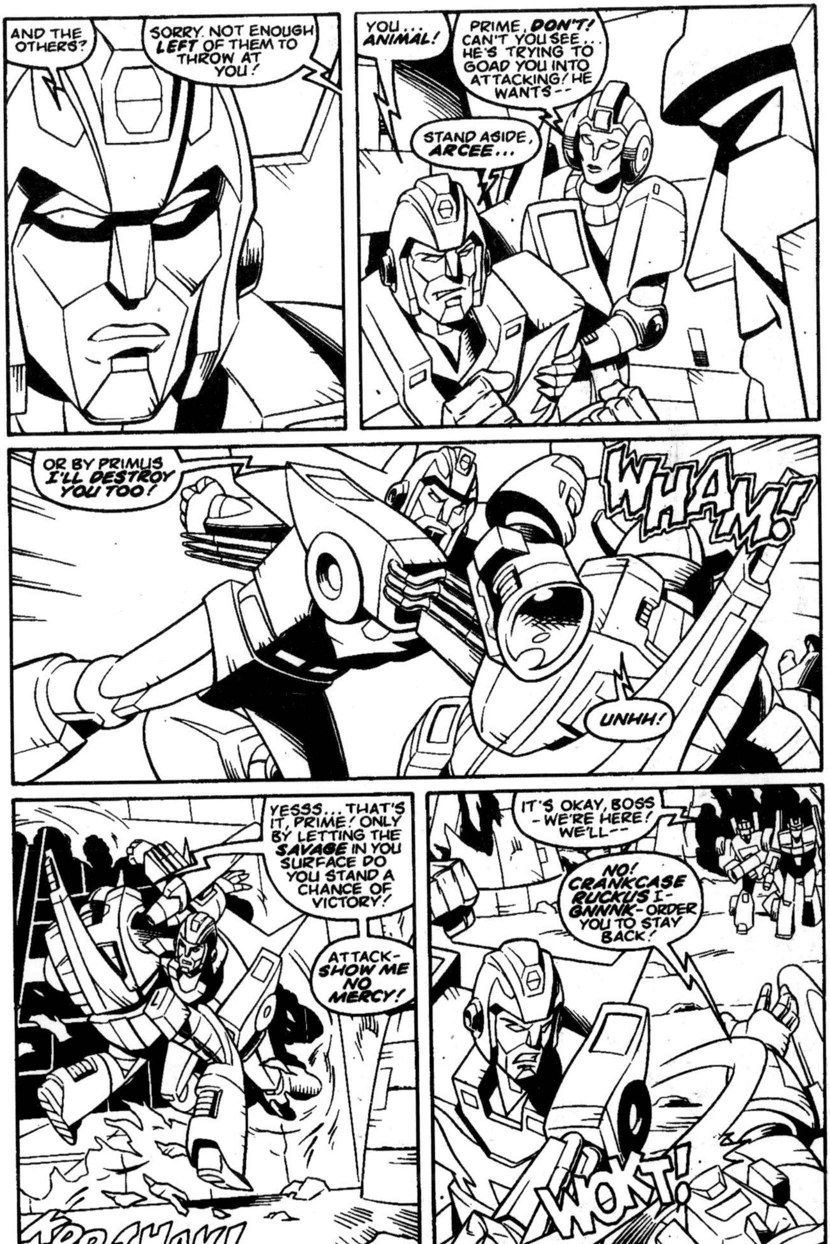
AND THE OTHERS?
SORRY. NOT ENOUGH LEFT OF THEM TO THROW AT YOU!
YOU... ANIMAL!
PRIME, DON'T! CAN'T YOU SEE... HE'S TRYING TO GOAD YOU INTO ATTACKING! HE WANTS--
STAND ASIDE, ARCEE...
OR BY PRIMUS I'LL DESTROY YOU TOO!
WHAM!
UNHH!
YESSS... THAT'S IT, PRIME! ONLY BY LETTING THE SAVAGE IN YOU SURFACE DO YOU STAND A CHANCE OF VICTORY!
ATTACK-SHOW ME NO MERCY!
KRR-CHAK!
IT'S OKAY, BOSS -WE'RE HERE! WE'LL--
NO! CRANKCASE RUCKUS I-GNNNK-ORDER YOU TO STAY BACK!
WOK'T!

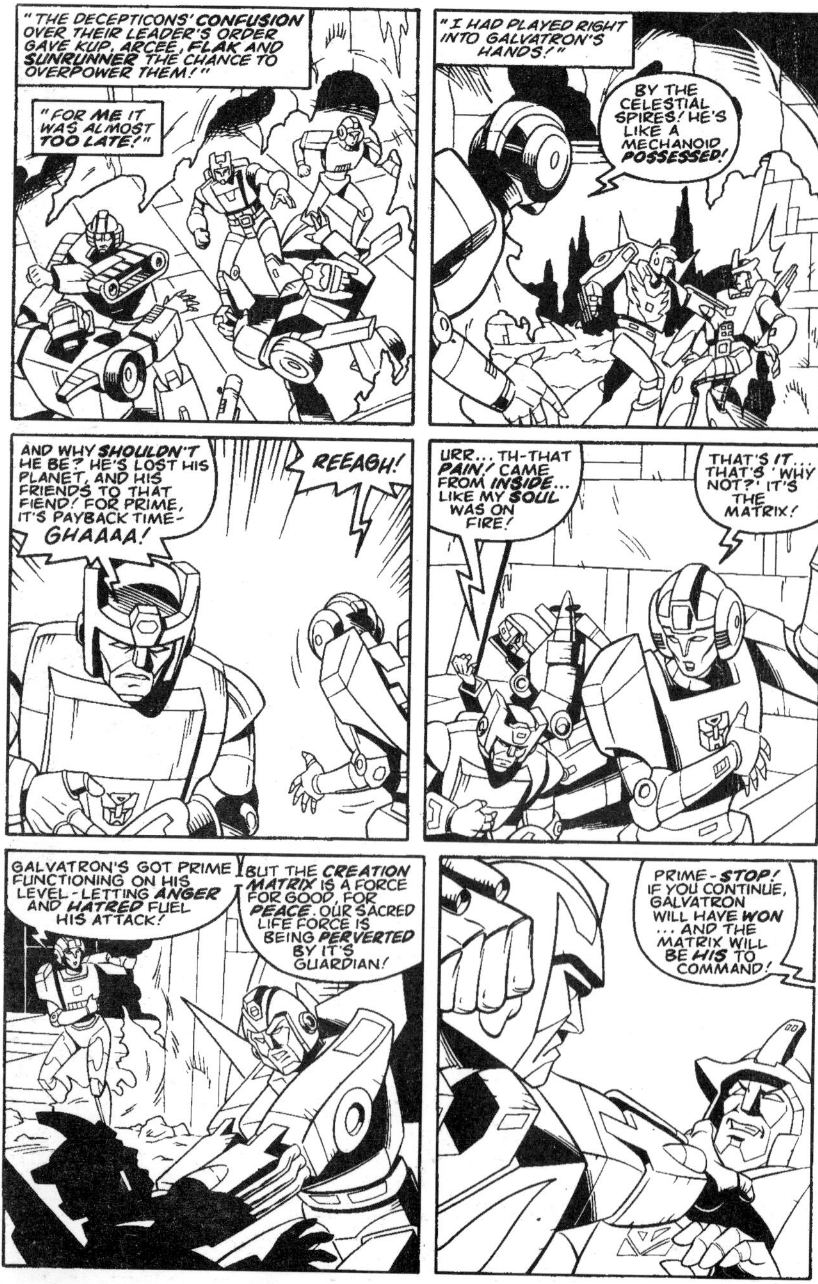
"THE DECEPTICONS' CONFUSION OVER THEIR LEADER'S ORDER GAVE KUP, ARCEE, FLAK AND SUNRUNNER THE CHANCE TO OVERPOWER THEM!"
"FOR ME IT WAS ALMOST TOO LATE!"
"I HAD PLAYED RIGHT INTO GALVATRON'S HANDS!"
BY THE CELESTIAL SPIRES! HE'S LIKE A MECHANOID POSSESSED!
AND WHY SHOULDN'T HE BE? HE'S LOST HIS PLANET, AND HIS FRIENDS TO THAT FIEND! FOR PRIME, IT'S PAYBACK TIME- GHAAAA!
REEAGH!
URR... TH-THAT PAIN! CAME FROM INSIDE... LIKE MY SOUL WAS ON FIRE!
THAT'S IT... THAT'S 'WHY NOT?' IT'S THE MATRIX!
GALVATRON'S GOT PRIME FUNCTIONING ON HIS LEVEL - LETTING ANGER AND HATRED FUEL HIS ATTACK!
BUT THE CREATION MATRIX IS A FORCE FOR GOOD, FOR PEACE. OUR SACRED LIFE FORCE IS BEING PERVERTED BY IT'S GUARDIAN!
PRIME - STOP! IF YOU CONTINUE, GALVATRON WILL HAVE WON ... AND THE MATRIX WILL BE HIS TO COMMAND!

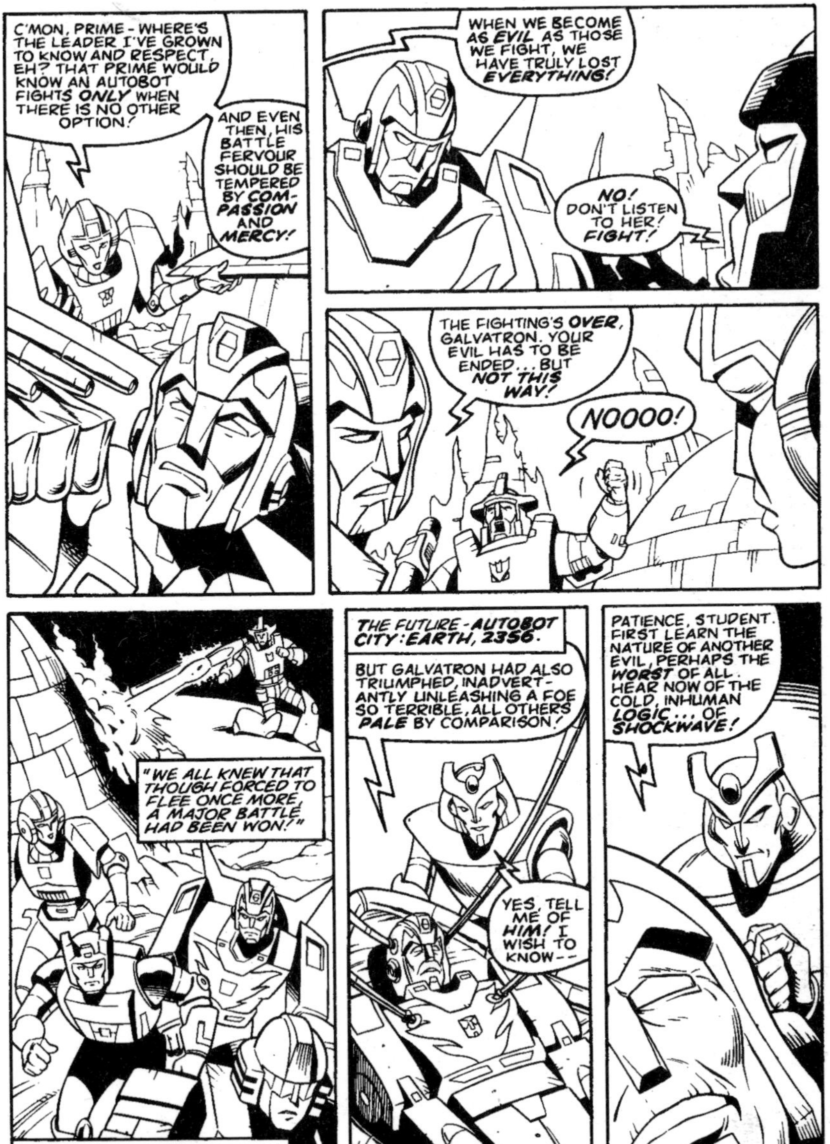
C'MON, PRIME - WHERE'S THE LEADER I'VE GROWN TO KNOW AND RESPECT, EH? THAT PRIME WOULD KNOW AN AUTOBOT FIGHTS ONLY WHEN THERE IS NO OTHER OPTION!
AND EVEN THEN, HIS BATTLE FERVOUR SHOULD BE TEMPERED BY COMPASSION AND MERCY!
WHEN WE BECOME AS EVIL AS THOSE WE FIGHT, WE HAVE TRULY LOST EVERYTHING!
NO! DON'T LISTEN TO HER! FIGHT!
THE FIGHTING'S OVER, GALVATRON. YOUR EVIL HAS TO BE ENDED... BUT NOT THIS WAY!
NOOOO!
"WE ALL KNEW THAT THOUGH FORCED TO FLEE ONCE MORE, A MAJOR BATTLE HAD BEEN WON!"
"WE'D FACED A SAVAGE EVIL ... AND TRIUMPHED OVER THE SAVAGE WITHIN US ALL!"
THE FUTURE - AUTOBOT CITY: EARTH, 2356.
BUT GALVATRON HAD ALSO TRIUMPHED, INADVERTANTLY UNLEASHING A FOE SO TERRIBLE, ALL OTHERS PALE BY COMPARISON!
YES, TELL ME OF HIM! I WISH TO KNOW--
PATIENCE, STUDENT. FIRST LEARN THE NATURE OF ANOTHER EVIL, PERHAPS THE WORST OF ALL. HEAR NOW OF THE COLD, INHUMAN LOGIC... OF SHOCKWAVE!

NEXT: SHOCKWAVE!

TRANSFORMERS™

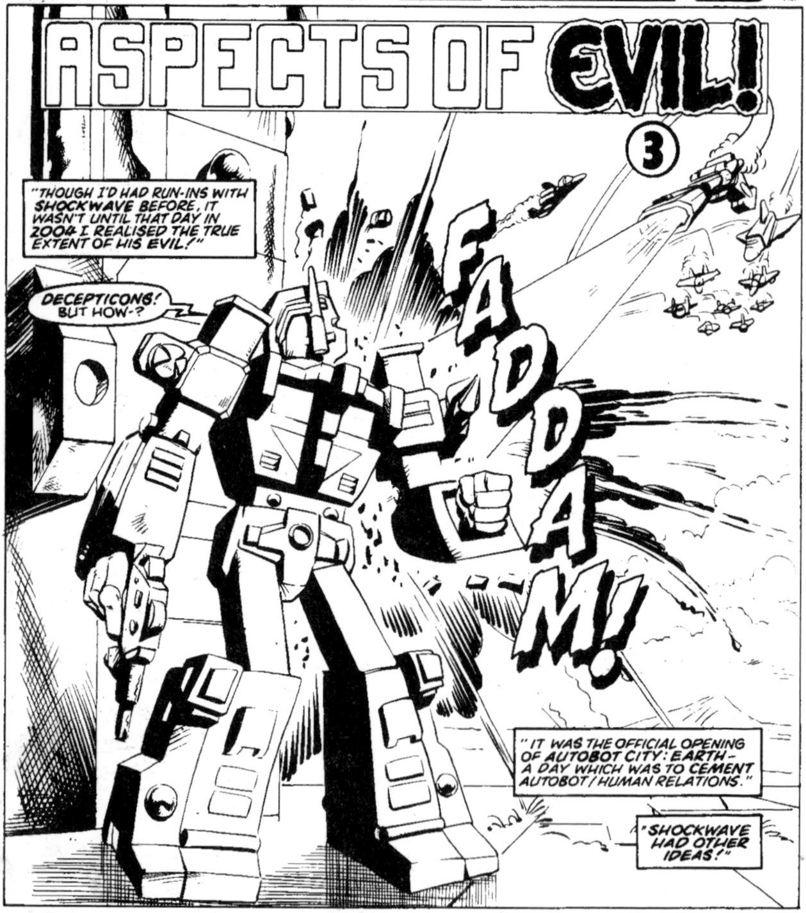
ASPECTS OF EVIL!
3
"THOUGH I'D HAD RUN-INS WITH SHOCKWAVE BEFORE, IT WASN'T UNTIL THAT DAY IN 2004 I REALISED THE TRUE EXTENT OF HIS EVIL!"
DECEPTICONS! BUT HOW-?
FADDAM!
"IT WAS THE OFFICIAL OPENING OF AUTOBOT CITY: EARTH - A DAY WHICH WAS TO CEMENT AUTOBOT/HUMAN RELATIONS."
"SHOCKWAVE HAD OTHER IDEAS!"

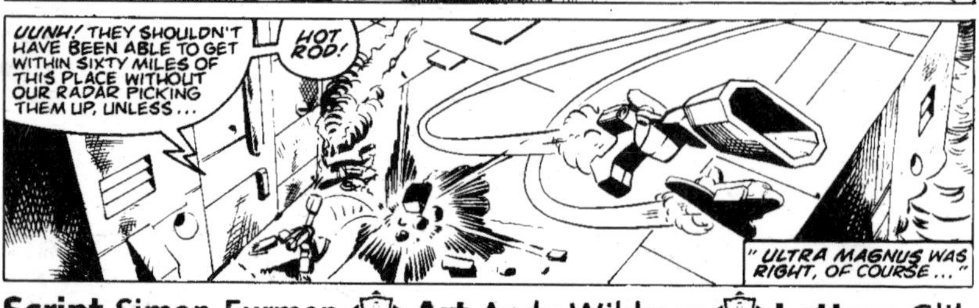
UUNH! THEY SHOULDN'T HAVE BEEN ABLE TO GET WITHIN SIXTY MILES OF THIS PLACE WITHOUT OUR RADAR PICKING THEM UP, UNLESS...
HOT ROD!
"ULTRA MAGNUS WAS RIGHT, OF COURSE..."

Script Simon Furman **Art** Andy Wildman **Letters** Glib

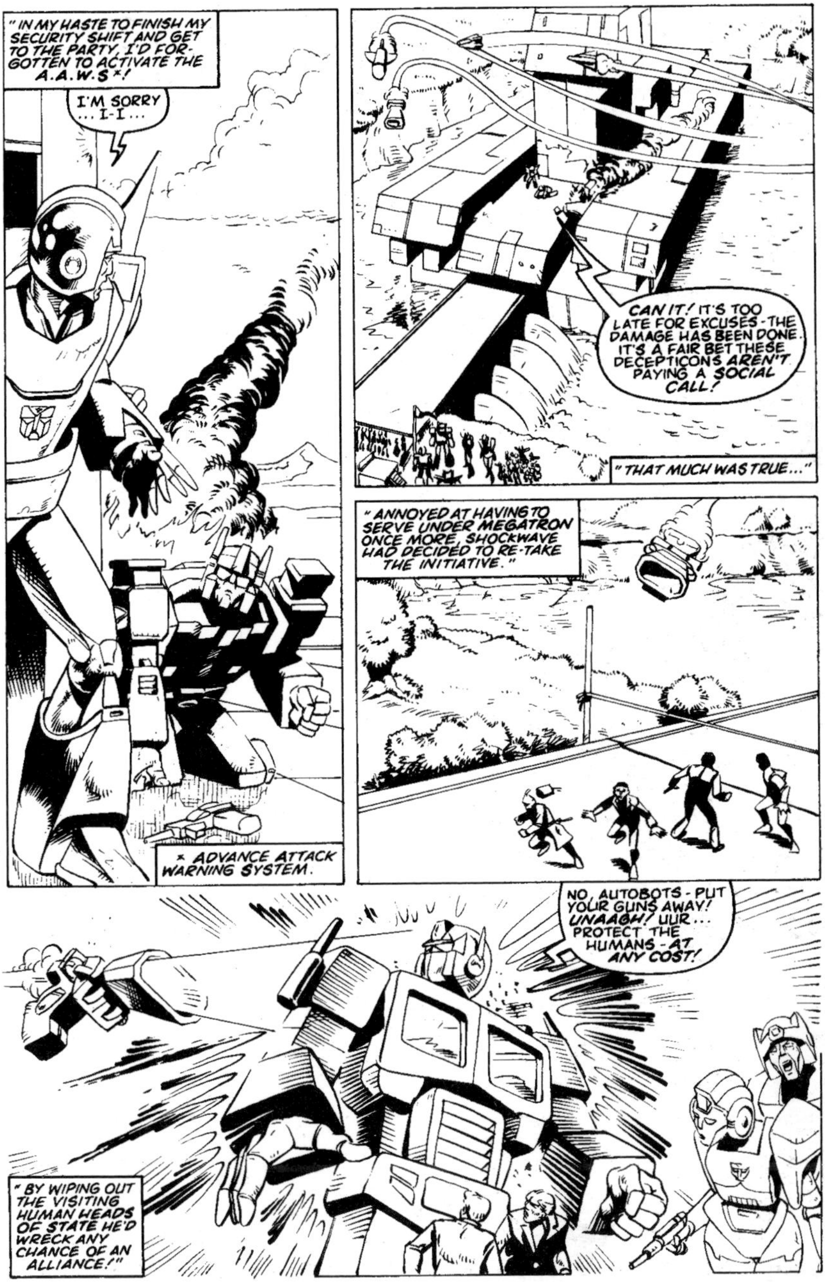
"IN MY HASTE TO FINISH MY SECURITY SHIFT AND GET TO THE PARTY, I'D FORGOTTEN TO ACTIVATE THE A.A.W.S*!
I'M SORRY ... I-I ...
* ADVANCE ATTACK WARNING SYSTEM.
CAN IT! IT'S TOO LATE FOR EXCUSES - THE DAMAGE HAS BEEN DONE. IT'S A FAIR BET THESE DECEPTICONS AREN'T PAYING A SOCIAL CALL!
"THAT MUCH WAS TRUE..."
"ANNOYED AT HAVING TO SERVE UNDER MEGATRON ONCE MORE, SHOCKWAVE HAD DECIDED TO RE-TAKE THE INITIATIVE."
NO, AUTOBOTS - PUT YOUR GUNS AWAY! UNAAGH! UUR... PROTECT THE HUMANS - AT ANY COST!
"BY WIPING OUT THE VISITING HUMAN HEADS OF STATE HE'D WRECK ANY CHANCE OF AN ALLIANCE!"

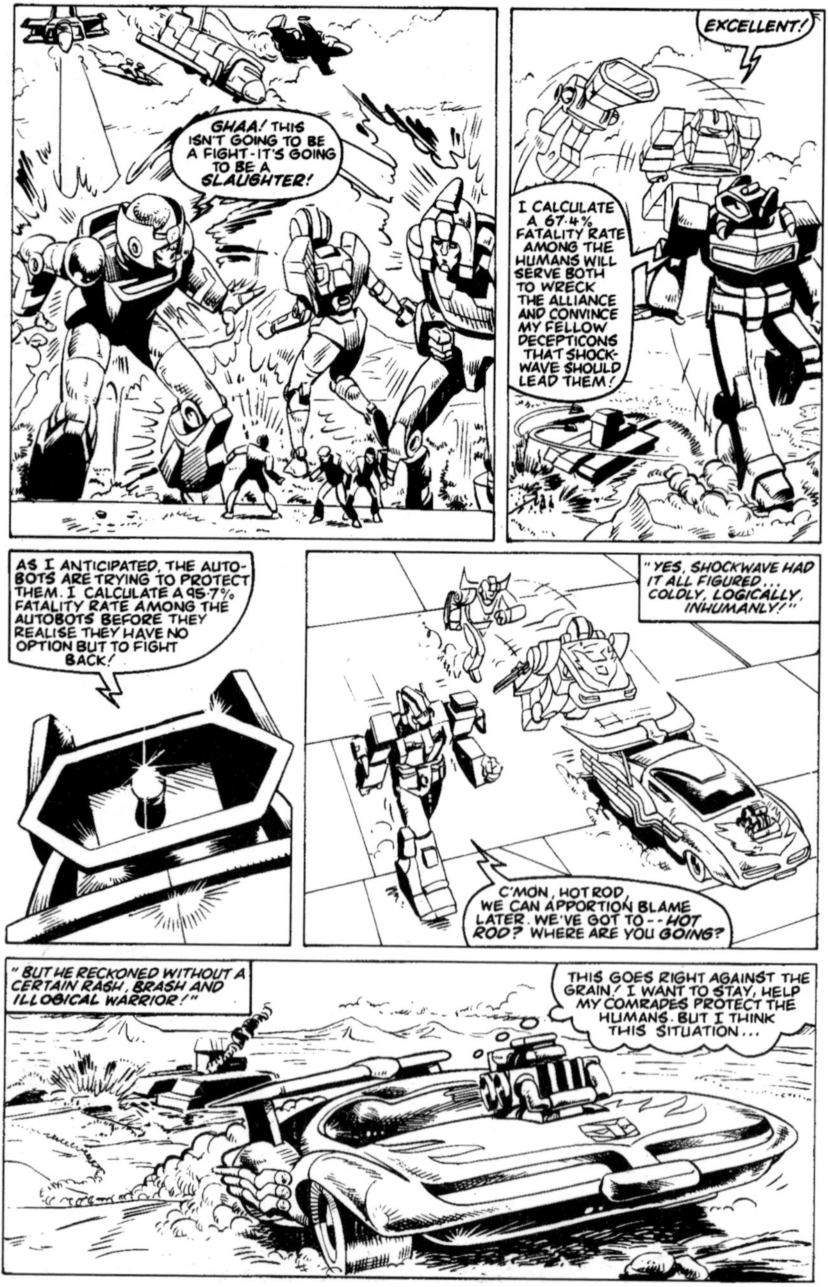
GHAA! THIS ISN'T GOING TO BE A FIGHT - IT'S GOING TO BE A SLAUGHTER!
EXCELLENT!
I CALCULATE A 67·4% FATALITY RATE AMONG THE HUMANS WILL SERVE BOTH TO WRECK THE ALLIANCE AND CONVINCE MY FELLOW DECEPTICONS THAT SHOCKWAVE SHOULD LEAD THEM!
AS I ANTICIPATED, THE AUTOBOTS ARE TRYING TO PROTECT THEM. I CALCULATE A 95·7% FATALITY RATE AMONG THE AUTOBOTS BEFORE THEY REALISE THEY HAVE NO OPTION BUT TO FIGHT BACK!
"YES, SHOCKWAVE HAD IT ALL FIGURED... COLDLY, LOGICALLY, INHUMANLY!"
C'MON, HOT ROD, WE CAN APPORTION BLAME LATER. WE'VE GOT TO - - HOT ROD? WHERE ARE YOU GOING?
"BUT HE RECKONED WITHOUT A CERTAIN RASH, BRASH AND ILLOGICAL WARRIOR!"
THIS GOES RIGHT AGAINST THE GRAIN! I WANT TO STAY, HELP MY COMRADES PROTECT THE HUMANS. BUT I THINK THIS SITUATION...

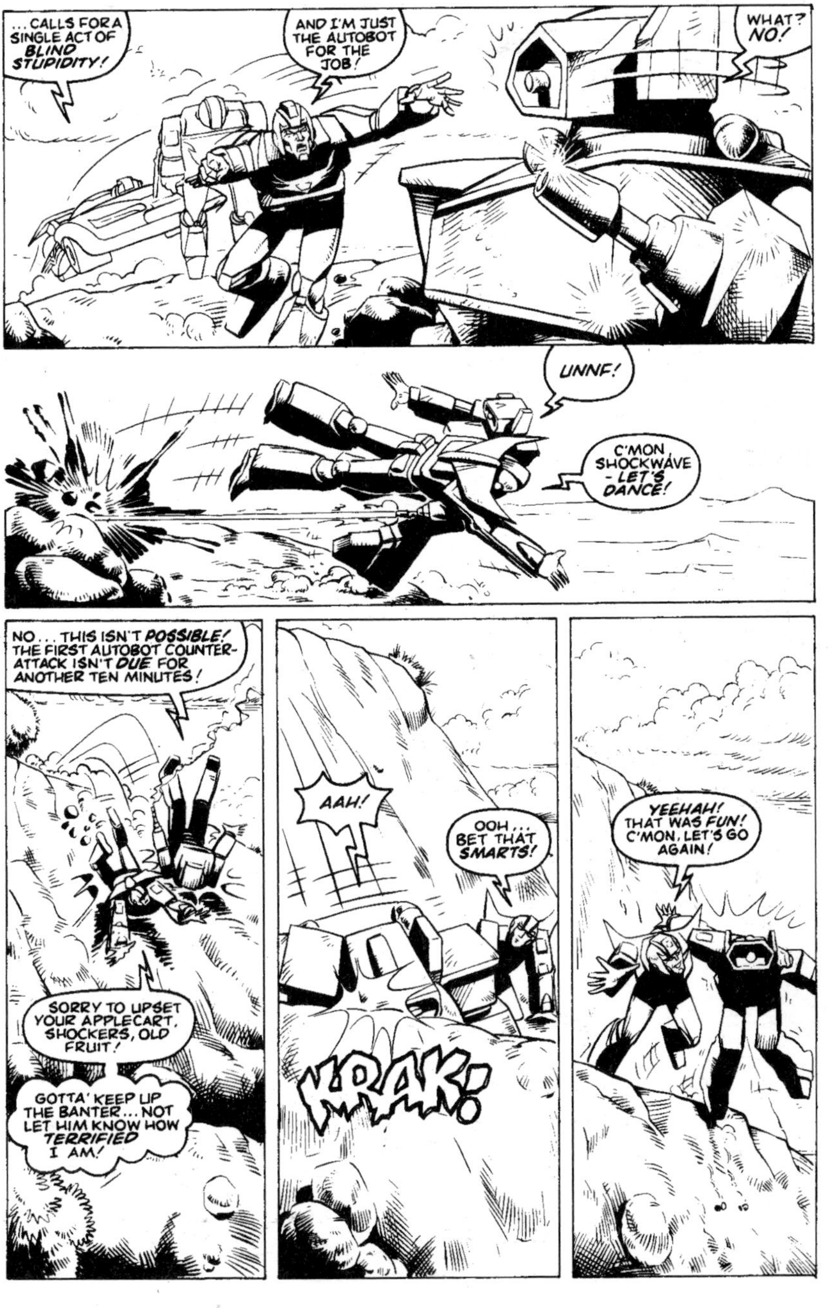
...CALLS FOR A SINGLE ACT OF BLIND STUPIDITY!
AND I'M JUST THE AUTOBOT FOR THE JOB!
WHAT? NO!
UNNF!
C'MON, SHOCKWAVE - LET'S DANCE!
NO... THIS ISN'T POSSIBLE! THE FIRST AUTOBOT COUNTER-ATTACK ISN'T DUE FOR ANOTHER TEN MINUTES!
SORRY TO UPSET YOUR APPLECART, SHOCKERS, OLD FRUIT!
GOTTA' KEEP UP THE BANTER... NOT LET HIM KNOW HOW TERRIFIED I AM!
AAH!
OOH... BET THAT SMARTS!
KRAK!
YEEHAH! THAT WAS FUN! C'MON, LET'S GO AGAIN!

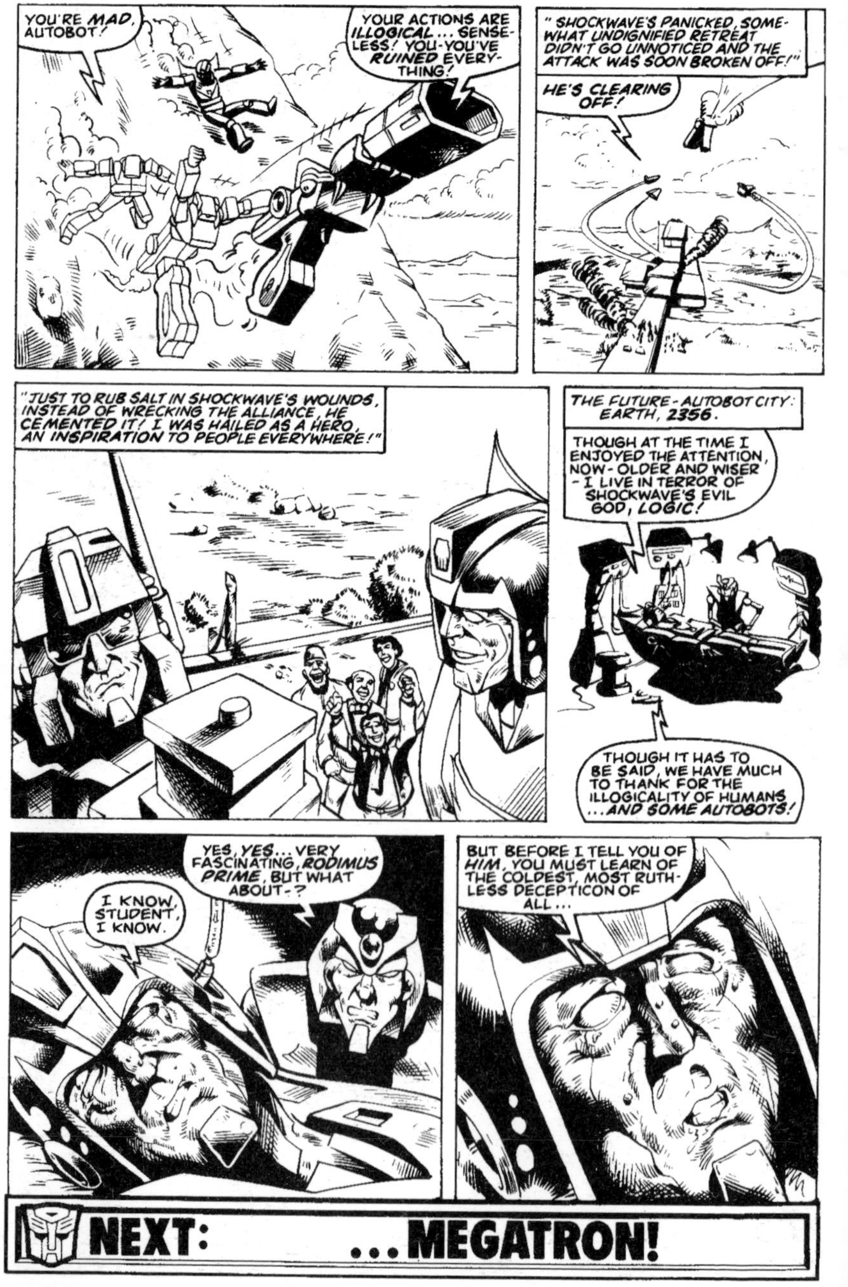

YOU'RE MAD, AUTOBOT!
YOUR ACTIONS ARE ILLOGICAL... SENSELESS! YOU-YOU'VE RUINED EVERYTHING!
"SHOCKWAVE'S PANICKED, SOMEWHAT UNDIGNIFIED RETREAT DIDN'T GO UNNOTICED AND THE ATTACK WAS SOON BROKEN OFF!"
HE'S CLEARING OFF!
"JUST TO RUB SALT IN SHOCKWAVE'S WOUNDS, INSTEAD OF WRECKING THE ALLIANCE, HE CEMENTED IT! I WAS HAILED AS A HERO, AN INSPIRATION TO PEOPLE EVERYWHERE!"
THE FUTURE - AUTOBOT CITY: EARTH, 2356.
THOUGH AT THE TIME I ENJOYED THE ATTENTION, NOW - OLDER AND WISER - I LIVE IN TERROR OF SHOCKWAVE'S EVIL GOD, LOGIC!
THOUGH IT HAS TO BE SAID, WE HAVE MUCH TO THANK FOR THE ILLOGICALITY OF HUMANS ...AND SOME AUTOBOTS!
YES, YES... VERY FASCINATING, RODIMUS PRIME, BUT WHAT ABOUT-?
I KNOW, STUDENT, I KNOW.
BUT BEFORE I TELL YOU OF HIM, YOU MUST LEARN OF THE COLDEST, MOST RUTHLESS DECEPTICON OF ALL...
NEXT: ...MEGATRON!

TRANSFORMERS™

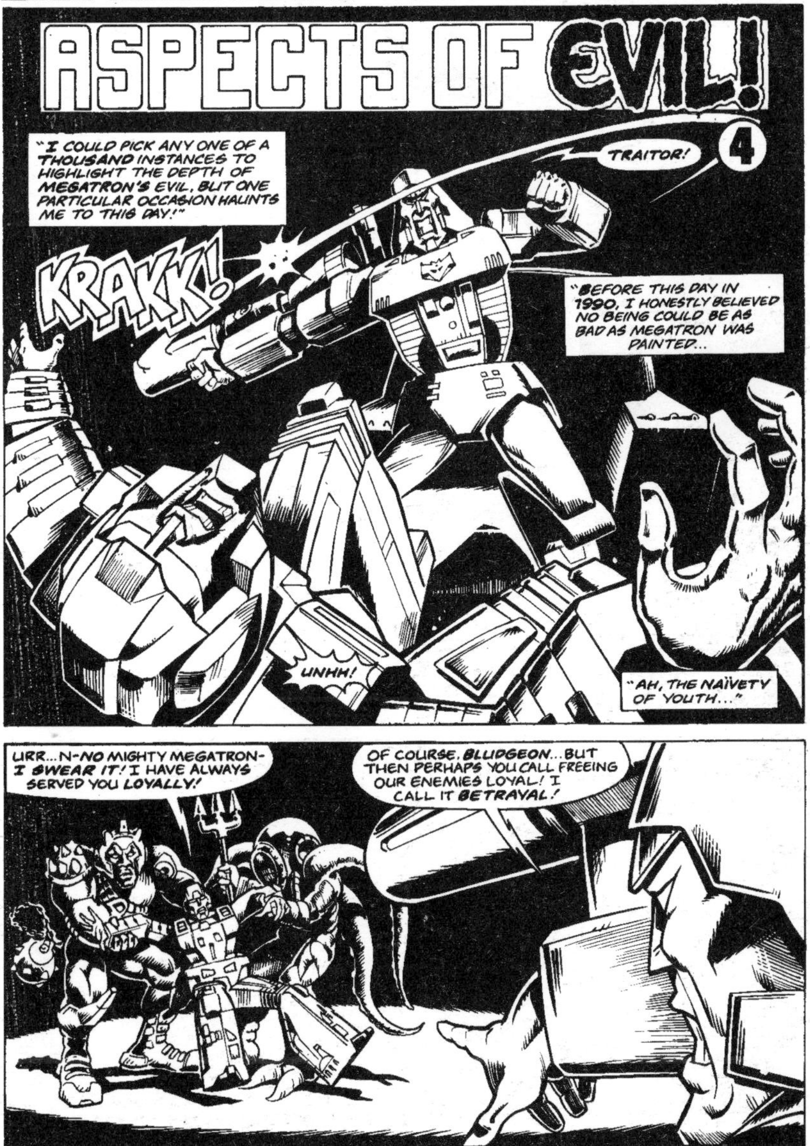
ASPECTS OF EVIL!
4
"I COULD PICK ANY ONE OF A THOUSAND INSTANCES TO HIGHLIGHT THE DEPTH OF MEGATRON'S EVIL, BUT ONE PARTICULAR OCCASION HAUNTS ME TO THIS DAY!"
TRAITOR!
KRAKK!
"BEFORE THIS DAY IN 1990, I HONESTLY BELIEVED NO BEING COULD BE AS BAD AS MEGATRON WAS PAINTED...
UNHH!
"AH, THE NAÏVETY OF YOUTH..."
URR... N-NO MIGHTY MEGATRON- I SWEAR IT! I HAVE ALWAYS SERVED YOU LOYALLY!
OF COURSE, BLUDGEON... BUT THEN PERHAPS YOU CALL FREEING OUR ENEMIES LOYAL! I CALL IT BETRAYAL!

Script Simon Furman **Art** Lee Sullivan **Letters** Nick Abadzis

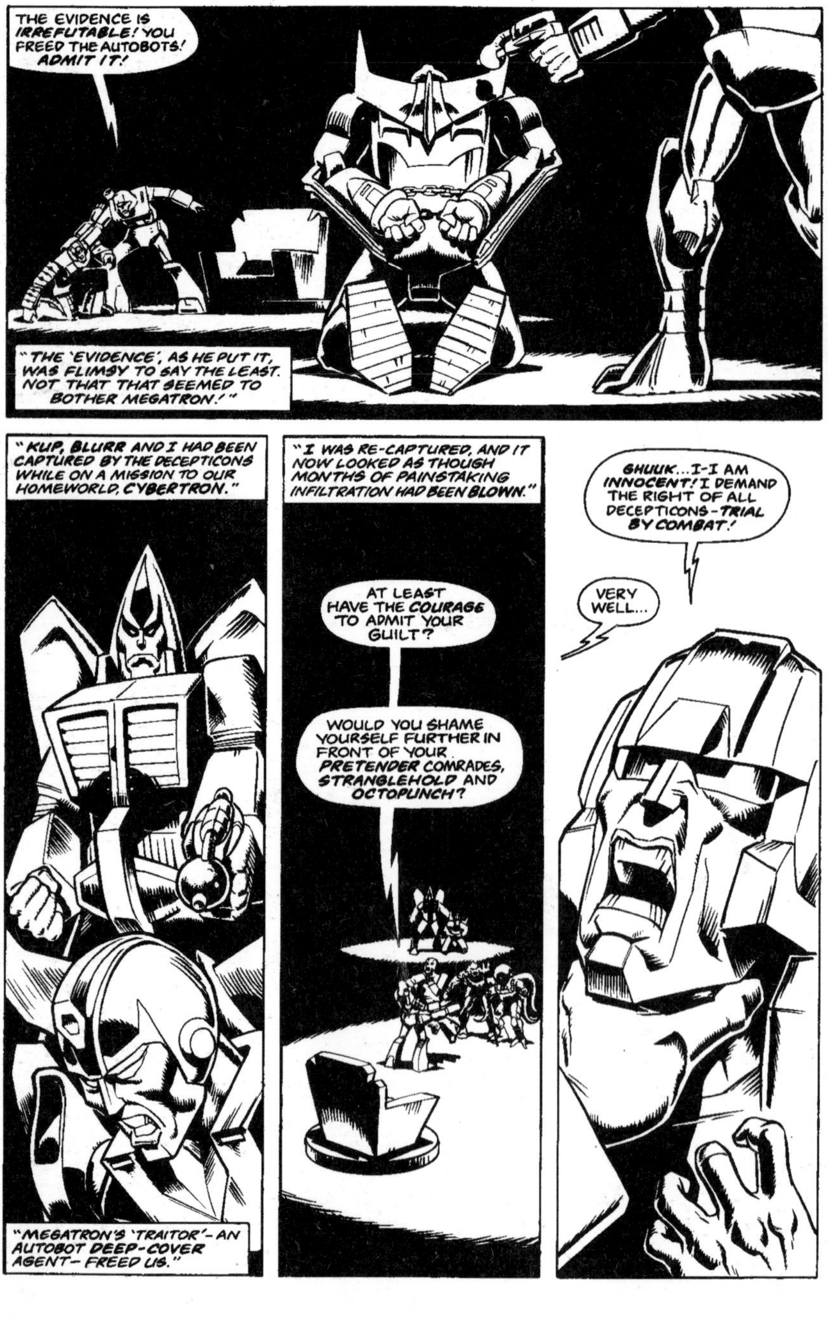
THE EVIDENCE IS IRREFUTABLE! YOU FREED THE AUTOBOTS! ADMIT IT!
"THE 'EVIDENCE', AS HE PUT IT, WAS FLIMSY TO SAY THE LEAST. NOT THAT THAT SEEMED TO BOTHER MEGATRON!"
"KUP, BLURR AND I HAD BEEN CAPTURED BY THE DECEPTICONS WHILE ON A MISSION TO OUR HOMEWORLD, CYBERTRON."
"MEGATRON'S 'TRAITOR'– AN AUTOBOT DEEP-COVER AGENT– FREED US."
"I WAS RE-CAPTURED, AND IT NOW LOOKED AS THOUGH MONTHS OF PAINSTAKING INFILTRATION HAD BEEN BLOWN."
AT LEAST HAVE THE COURAGE TO ADMIT YOUR GUILT?
WOULD YOU SHAME YOURSELF FURTHER IN FRONT OF YOUR PRETENDER COMRADES, STRANGLEHOLD AND OCTOPUNCH?
GHUUK... I-I AM INNOCENT! I DEMAND THE RIGHT OF ALL DECEPTICONS– TRIAL BY COMBAT!
VERY WELL...

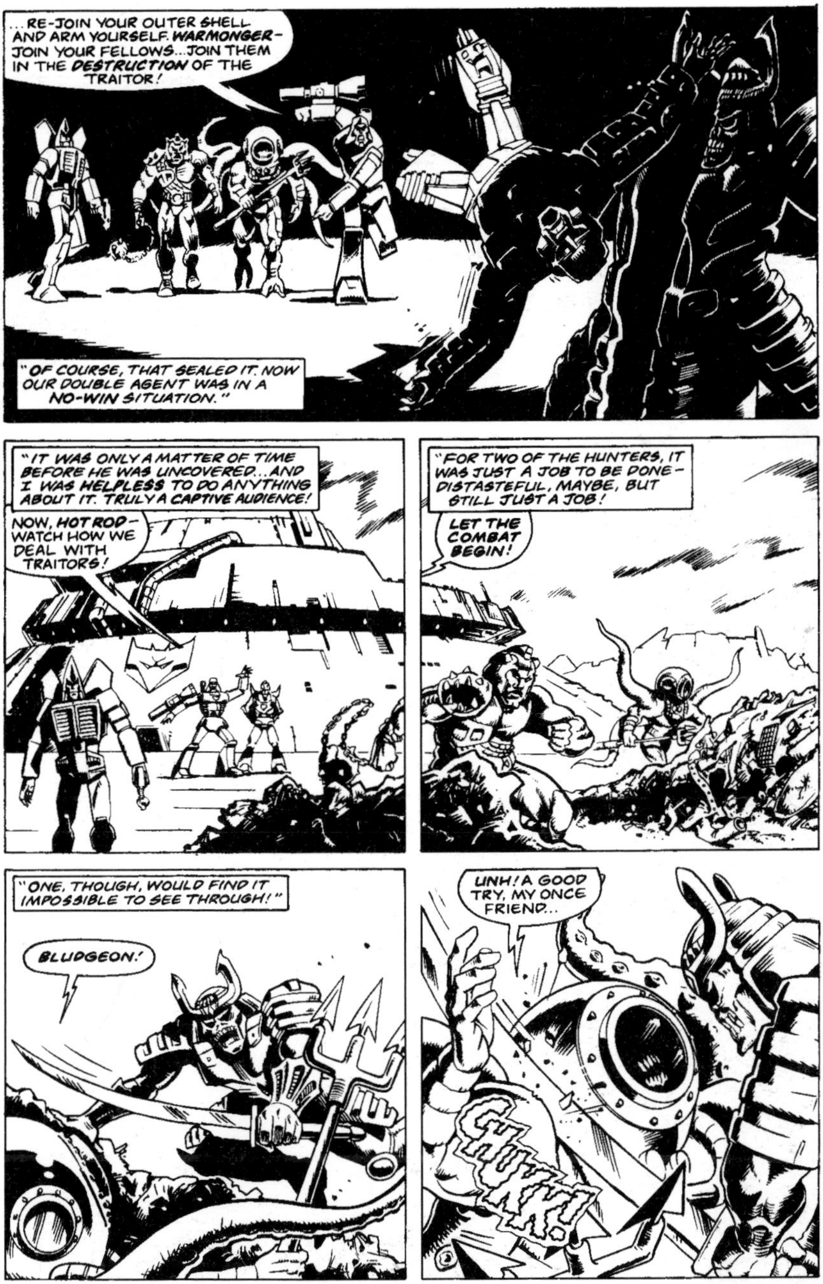
...RE-JOIN YOUR OUTER SHELL AND ARM YOURSELF. WARMONGER- JOIN YOUR FELLOWS...JOIN THEM IN THE DESTRUCTION OF THE TRAITOR!
"OF COURSE, THAT SEALED IT. NOW OUR DOUBLE AGENT WAS IN A NO-WIN SITUATION."
"IT WAS ONLY A MATTER OF TIME BEFORE HE WAS UNCOVERED...AND I WAS HELPLESS TO DO ANYTHING ABOUT IT. TRULY A CAPTIVE AUDIENCE!
NOW, HOT ROD- WATCH HOW WE DEAL WITH TRAITORS!
"FOR TWO OF THE HUNTERS, IT WAS JUST A JOB TO BE DONE- DISTASTEFUL, MAYBE, BUT STILL JUST A JOB!
LET THE COMBAT BEGIN!
"ONE, THOUGH, WOULD FIND IT IMPOSSIBLE TO SEE THROUGH!"
BLUDGEON!
UNH! A GOOD TRY, MY ONCE FRIEND...
GUK!

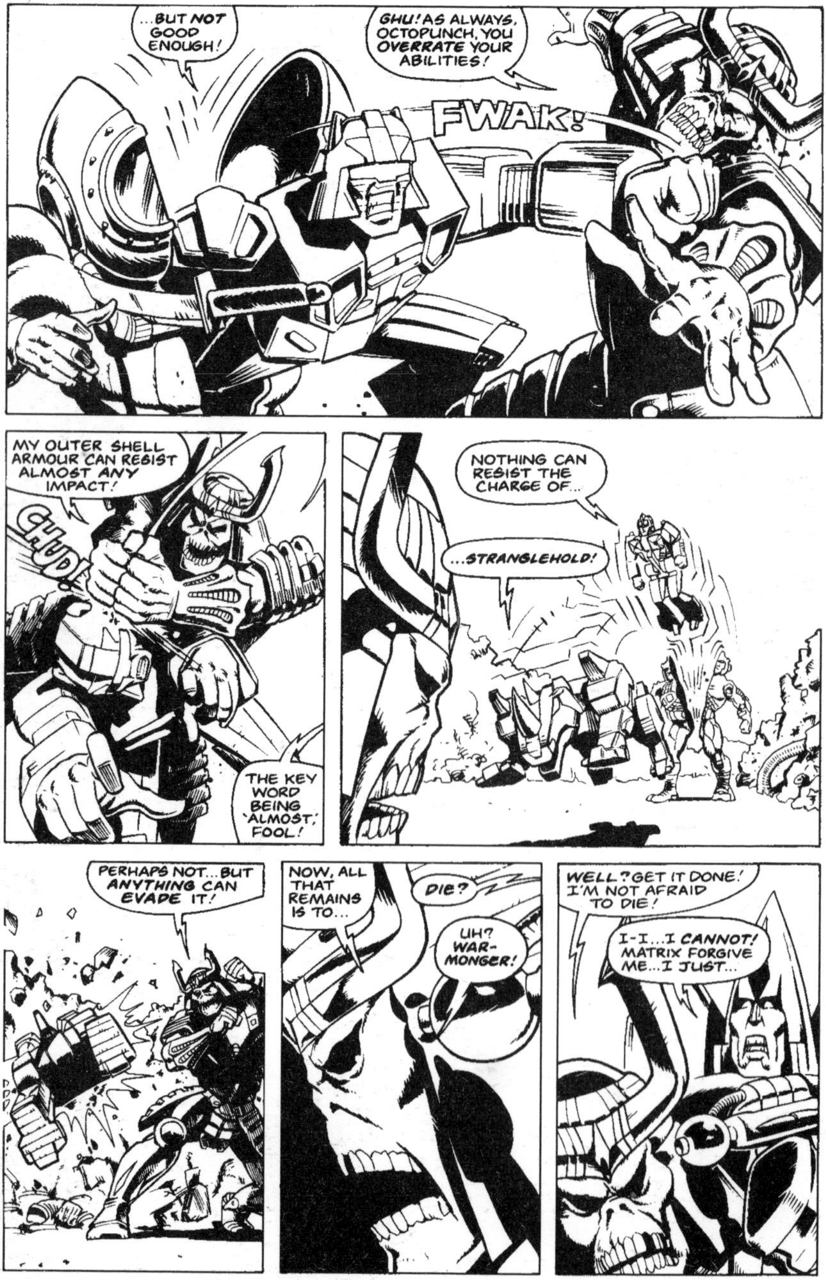
...BUT NOT GOOD ENOUGH!
GHU! AS ALWAYS, OCTOPUNCH, YOU OVERRATE YOUR ABILITIES!
FWAK!
MY OUTER SHELL ARMOUR CAN RESIST ALMOST ANY IMPACT!
CHUD!
THE KEY WORD BEING 'ALMOST,' FOOL!
NOTHING CAN RESIST THE CHARGE OF...
...STRANGLEHOLD!
PERHAPS NOT...BUT ANYTHING CAN EVADE IT!
NOW, ALL THAT REMAINS IS TO...
DIE?
UH? WAR-MONGER!
WELL? GET IT DONE! I'M NOT AFRAID TO DIE!
I-I...I CANNOT! MATRIX FORGIVE ME...I JUST...

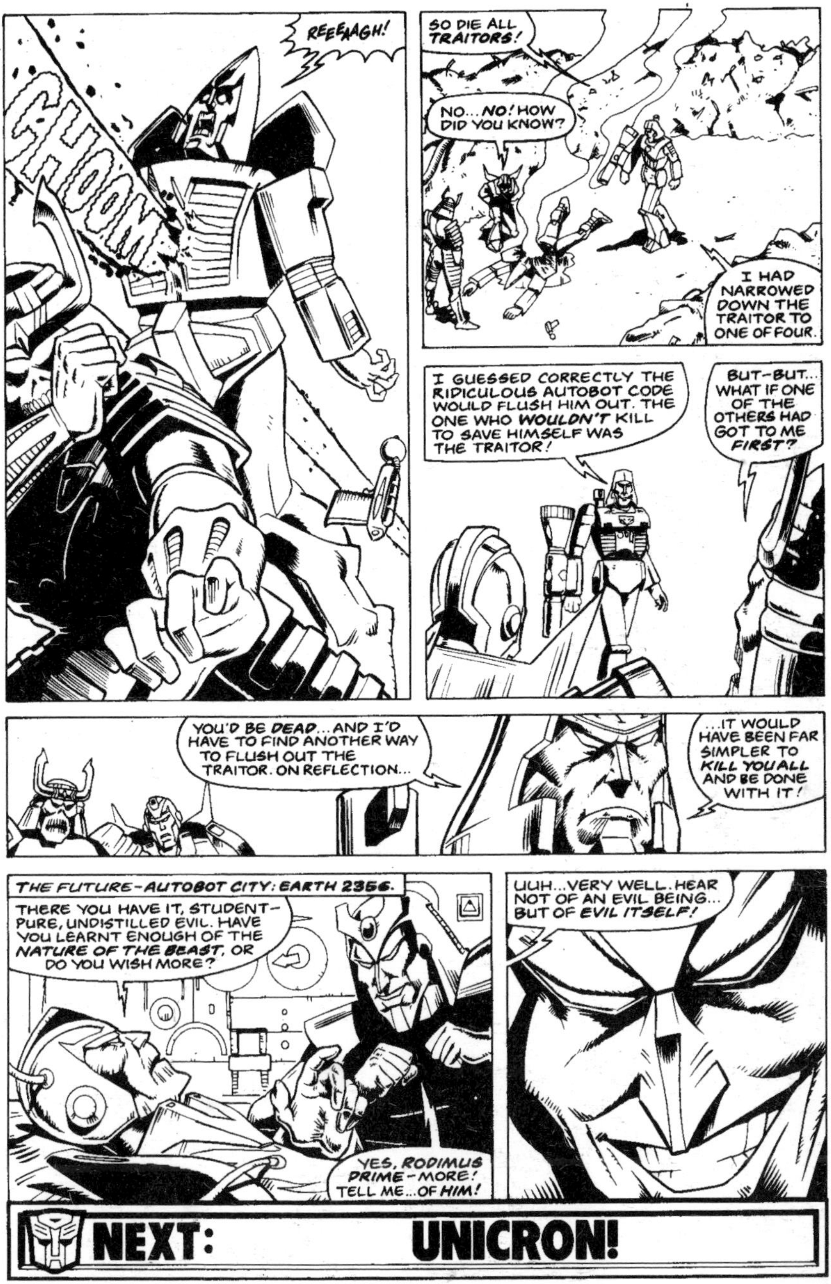
REEEAAGH!
CHOOM
SO DIE ALL TRAITORS!
NO... NO! HOW DID YOU KNOW?
I HAD NARROWED DOWN THE TRAITOR TO ONE OF FOUR.
I GUESSED CORRECTLY THE RIDICULOUS AUTOBOT CODE WOULD FLUSH HIM OUT. THE ONE WHO WOULDN'T KILL TO SAVE HIMSELF WAS THE TRAITOR!
BUT-BUT... WHAT IF ONE OF THE OTHERS HAD GOT TO ME FIRST?
YOU'D BE DEAD... AND I'D HAVE TO FIND ANOTHER WAY TO FLUSH OUT THE TRAITOR. ON REFLECTION...
...IT WOULD HAVE BEEN FAR SIMPLER TO KILL YOU ALL AND BE DONE WITH IT!
THE FUTURE- AUTOBOT CITY: EARTH 2356.
THERE YOU HAVE IT, STUDENT- PURE, UNDISTILLED EVIL. HAVE YOU LEARNT ENOUGH OF THE NATURE OF THE BEAST, OR DO YOU WISH MORE?
YES, RODIMUS PRIME- MORE! TELL ME... OF HIM!
UUH... VERY WELL. HEAR NOT OF AN EVIL BEING... BUT OF EVIL ITSELF!
NEXT: UNICRON!

TRANSFORMERS™

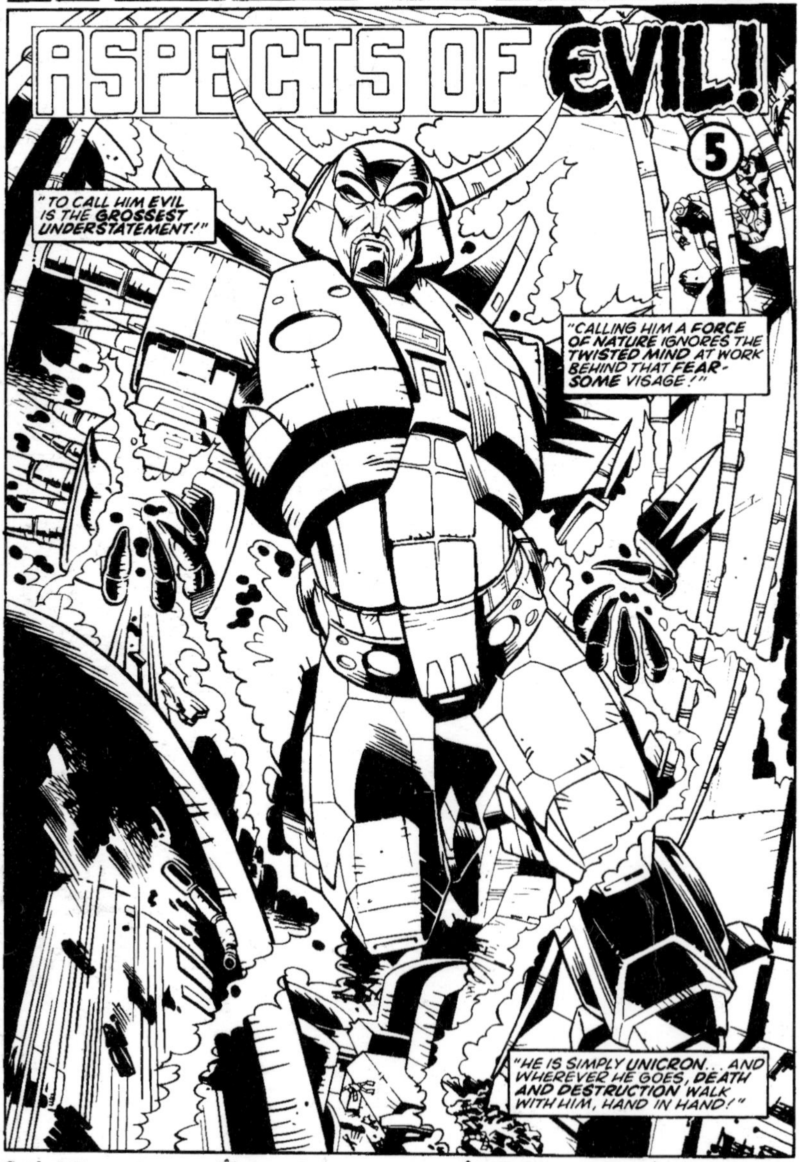
ASPECTS OF EVIL!
5
"TO CALL HIM EVIL IS THE GROSSEST UNDERSTATEMENT!"
"CALLING HIM A FORCE OF NATURE IGNORES THE TWISTED MIND AT WORK BEHIND THAT FEAR-SOME VISAGE!"
"HE IS SIMPLY UNICRON... AND WHEREVER HE GOES, DEATH AND DESTRUCTION WALK WITH HIM, HAND IN HAND!"

Script Simon Furman **Pencils** Simon Coleby **Inks** Cam Smith **Letters** Glib

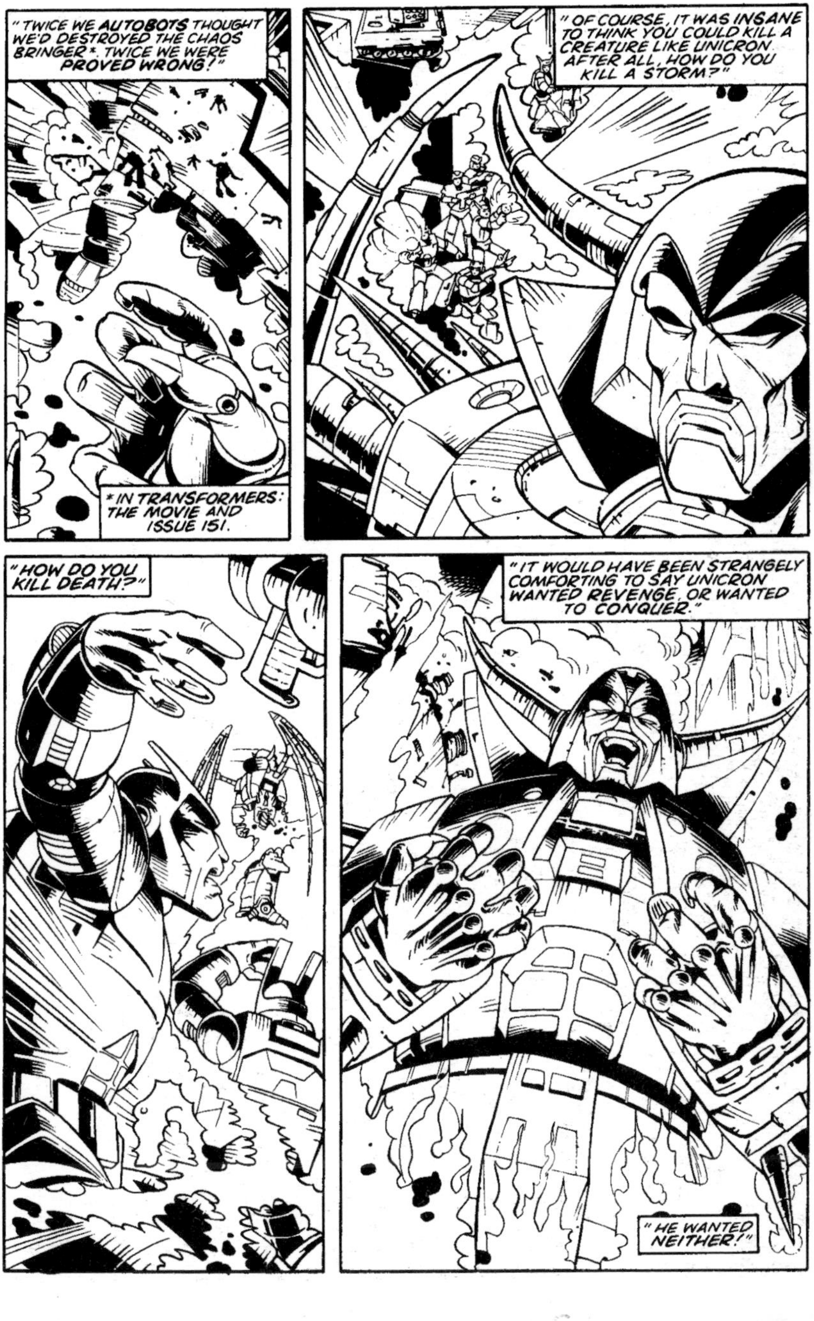
"TWICE WE AUTOBOTS THOUGHT WE'D DESTROYED THE CHAOS BRINGER*. TWICE WE WERE PROVED WRONG!"
*IN TRANSFORMERS: THE MOVIE AND ISSUE 151.
"OF COURSE, IT WAS INSANE TO THINK YOU COULD KILL A CREATURE LIKE UNICRON. AFTER ALL, HOW DO YOU KILL A STORM?"
"HOW DO YOU KILL DEATH?"
"IT WOULD HAVE BEEN STRANGELY COMFORTING TO SAY UNICRON WANTED REVENGE, OR WANTED TO CONQUER."
"HE WANTED NEITHER!"

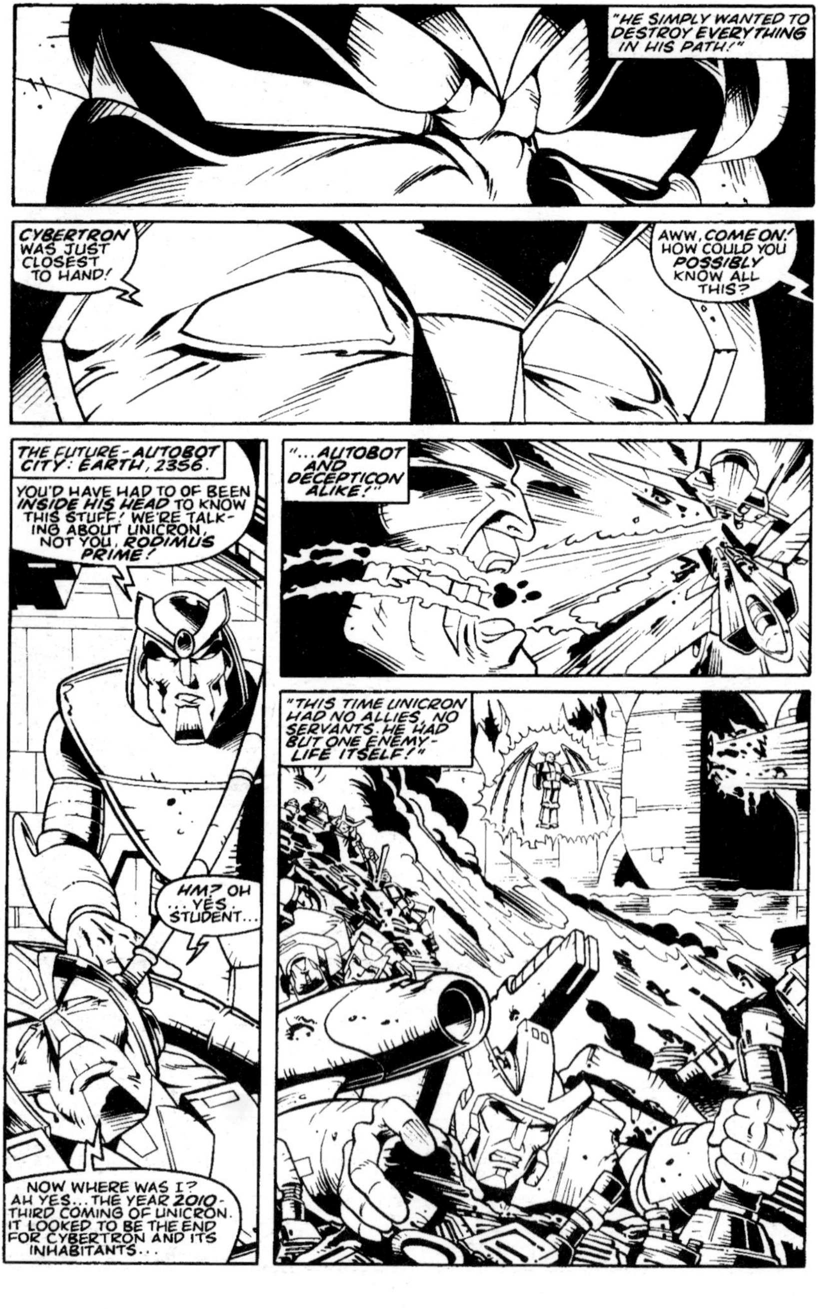
"HE SIMPLY WANTED TO DESTROY EVERYTHING IN HIS PATH!"
CYBERTRON WAS JUST CLOSEST TO HAND!
AWW, COME ON! HOW COULD YOU POSSIBLY KNOW ALL THIS?
THE FUTURE - AUTOBOT CITY: EARTH, 2356.
YOU'D HAVE HAD TO OF BEEN INSIDE HIS HEAD TO KNOW THIS STUFF! WE'RE TALKING ABOUT UNICRON, NOT YOU, RODIMUS PRIME!
HM? OH ... YES, STUDENT...
NOW WHERE WAS I? AH YES... THE YEAR 2010 - THIRD COMING OF UNICRON. IT LOOKED TO BE THE END FOR CYBERTRON AND ITS INHABITANTS...
"...AUTOBOT AND DECEPTICON ALIKE!"
"THIS TIME UNICRON HAD NO ALLIES, NO SERVANTS. HE HAD BUT ONE ENEMY - LIFE ITSELF!"

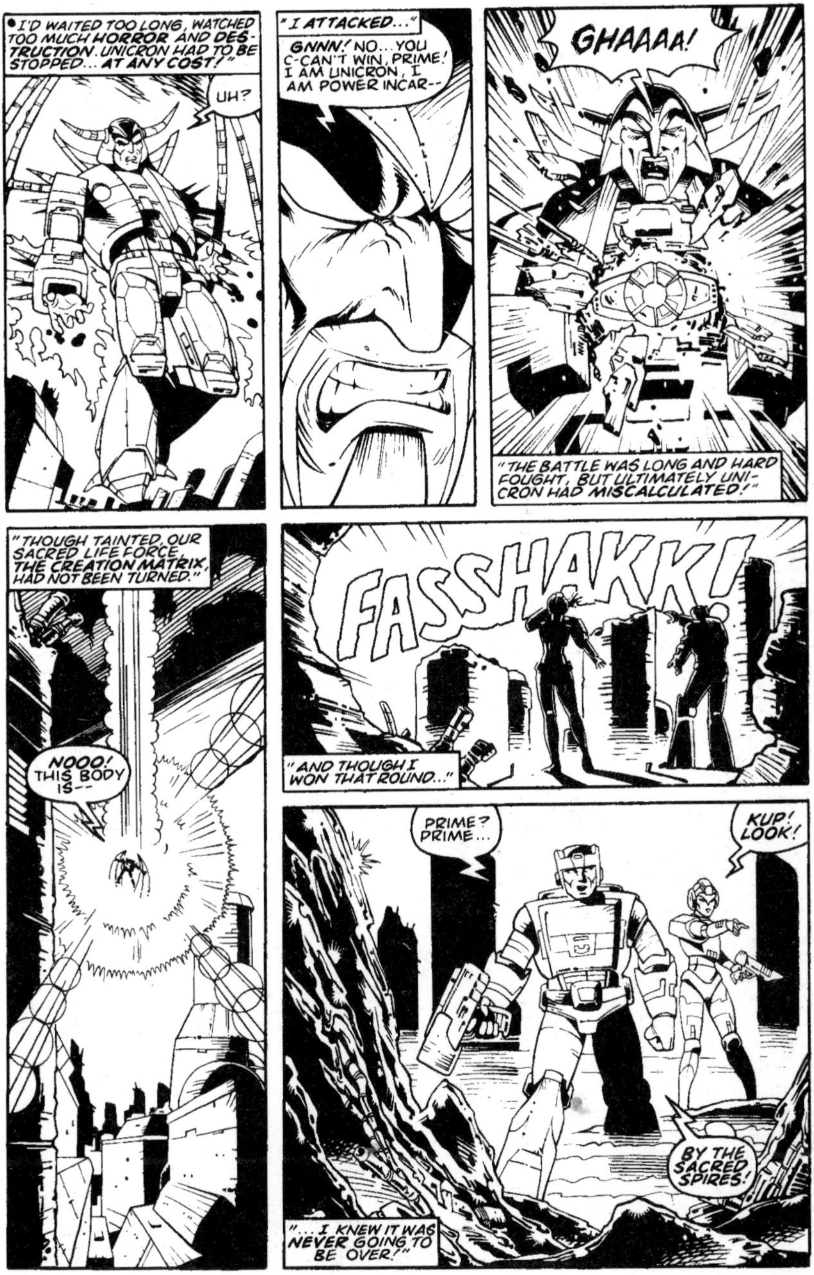
"I'D WAITED TOO LONG, WATCHED TOO MUCH HORROR AND DESTRUCTION. UNICRON HAD TO BE STOPPED... AT ANY COST!"
UH?
"I ATTACKED..."
GNNN! NO... YOU C-CAN'T WIN, PRIME! I AM UNICRON, I AM POWER INCAR--
GHAAAA!
"THE BATTLE WAS LONG AND HARD FOUGHT, BUT ULTIMATELY UNICRON HAD MISCALCULATED!"
"THOUGH TAINTED, OUR SACRED LIFE FORCE, THE CREATION MATRIX, HAD NOT BEEN TURNED."
NOOO! THIS BODY IS--
FASSHAKK!
"AND THOUGH I WON THAT ROUND..."
PRIME? PRIME...
KUP! LOOK!
BY THE SACRED SPIRES!
"...I KNEW IT WAS NEVER GOING TO BE OVER!"

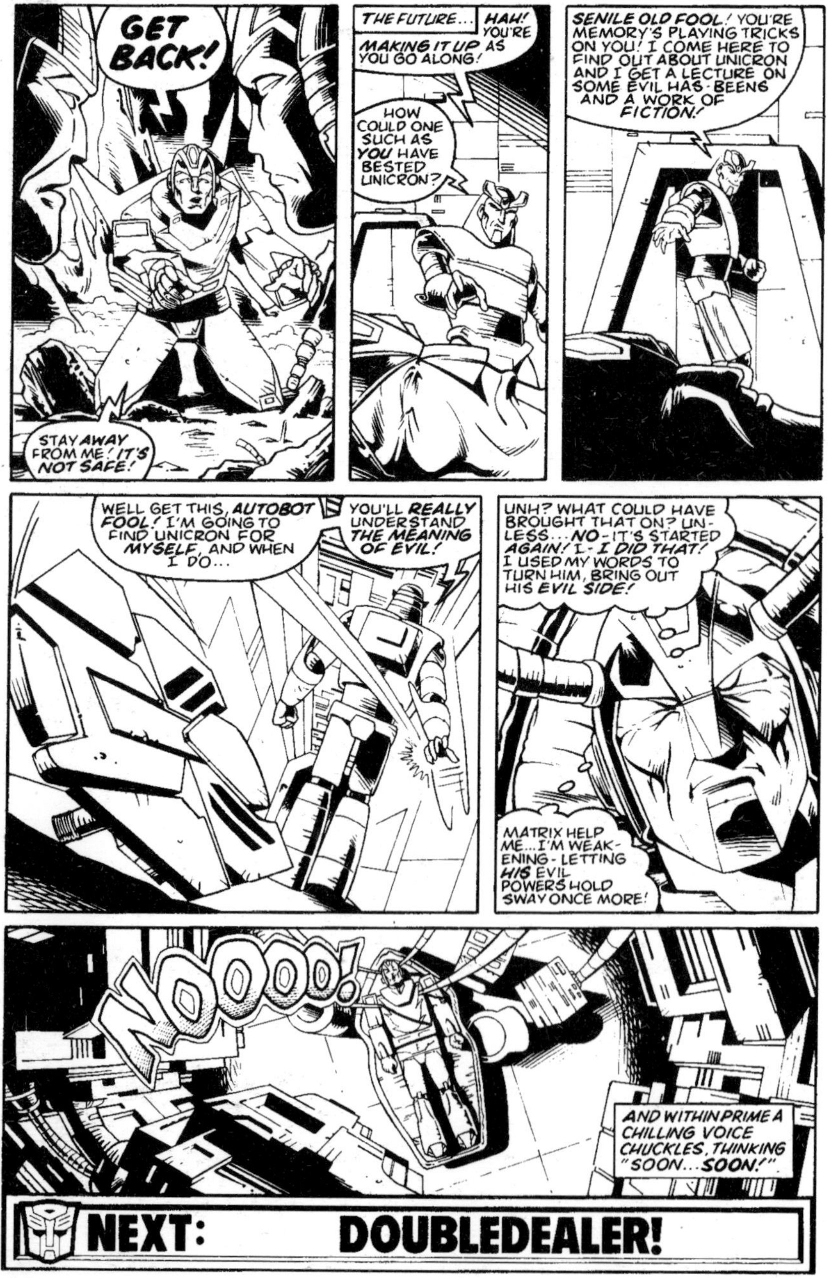
GET BACK!
STAY AWAY FROM ME! IT'S NOT SAFE!
THE FUTURE...
HAH! YOU'RE MAKING IT UP AS YOU GO ALONG!
HOW COULD ONE SUCH AS YOU HAVE BESTED UNICRON?
SENILE OLD FOOL! YOU'RE MEMORY'S PLAYING TRICKS ON YOU! I COME HERE TO FIND OUT ABOUT UNICRON AND I GET A LECTURE ON SOME EVIL HAS-BEENS AND A WORK OF FICTION!
WELL GET THIS, AUTOBOT FOOL! I'M GOING TO FIND UNICRON FOR MYSELF, AND WHEN I DO...
YOU'LL REALLY UNDERSTAND THE MEANING OF EVIL!
UNH? WHAT COULD HAVE BROUGHT THAT ON? UNLESS... NO - IT'S STARTED AGAIN! I - I DID THAT! I USED MY WORDS TO TURN HIM, BRING OUT HIS EVIL SIDE!
MATRIX HELP ME... I'M WEAKENING - LETTING HIS EVIL POWERS HOLD SWAY ONCE MORE!
NOOOOO!
AND WITHIN PRIME A CHILLING VOICE CHUCKLES, THINKING "SOON... SOON!"
NEXT: DOUBLEDEALER!

TRANSFORMERS™

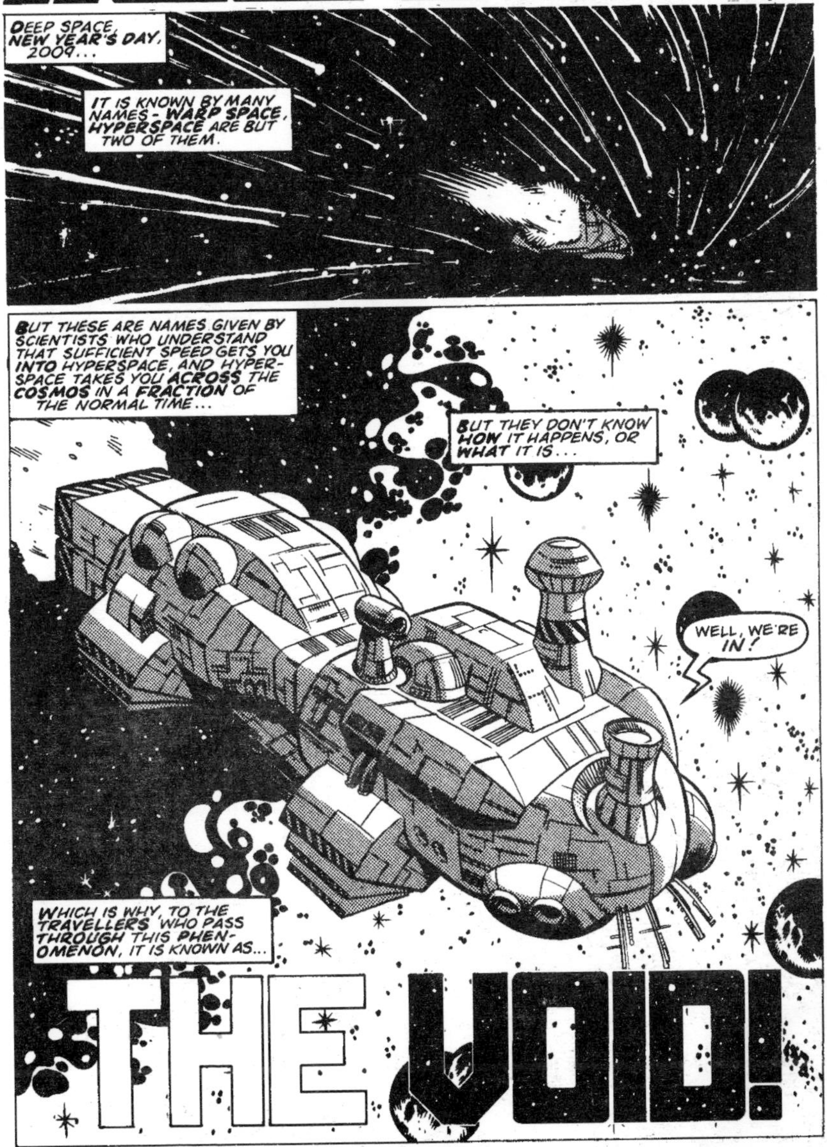
DEEP SPACE, NEW YEAR'S DAY, 2009...
IT IS KNOWN BY MANY NAMES - WARP SPACE, HYPERSPACE ARE BUT TWO OF THEM.
BUT THESE ARE NAMES GIVEN BY SCIENTISTS WHO UNDERSTAND THAT SUFFICIENT SPEED GETS YOU INTO HYPERSPACE, AND HYPER-SPACE TAKES YOU ACROSS THE COSMOS IN A FRACTION OF THE NORMAL TIME...
BUT THEY DON'T KNOW HOW IT HAPPENS, OR WHAT IT IS...
WELL, WE'RE IN!
WHICH IS WHY, TO THE TRAVELLERS WHO PASS THROUGH THIS PHEN-OMENON, IT IS KNOWN AS...
THE VOID!

Script Simon Furman **Art** Staz **Letters** Glib

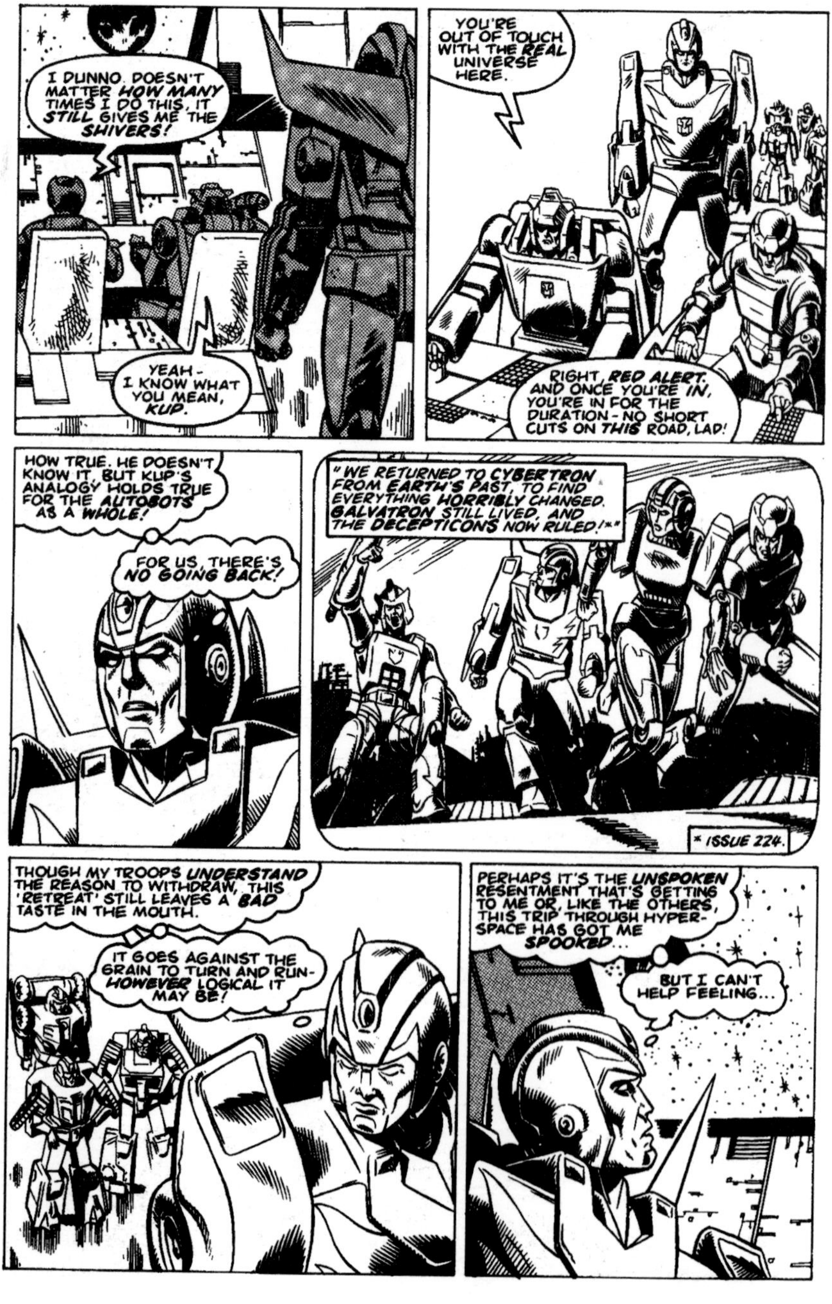
I DUNNO. DOESN'T MATTER HOW MANY TIMES I DO THIS, IT STILL GIVES ME THE SHIVERS!
YEAH - I KNOW WHAT YOU MEAN, KUP.
YOU'RE OUT OF TOUCH WITH THE REAL UNIVERSE HERE.
RIGHT, RED ALERT. AND ONCE YOU'RE IN, YOU'RE IN FOR THE DURATION - NO SHORT CUTS ON THIS ROAD, LAD!
HOW TRUE. HE DOESN'T KNOW IT, BUT KUP'S ANALOGY HOLDS TRUE FOR THE AUTOBOTS AS A WHOLE!
FOR US, THERE'S NO GOING BACK!
"WE RETURNED TO CYBERTRON FROM EARTH'S PAST, TO FIND EVERYTHING HORRIBLY CHANGED. GALVATRON STILL LIVED, AND THE DECEPTICONS NOW RULED!*"
* ISSUE 224.
THOUGH MY TROOPS UNDERSTAND THE REASON TO WITHDRAW, THIS 'RETREAT' STILL LEAVES A BAD TASTE IN THE MOUTH.
IT GOES AGAINST THE GRAIN TO TURN AND RUN - HOWEVER LOGICAL IT MAY BE!
PERHAPS IT'S THE UNSPOKEN RESENTMENT THAT'S GETTING TO ME OR, LIKE THE OTHERS, THIS TRIP THROUGH HYPER-SPACE HAS GOT ME SPOOKED...
BUT I CAN'T HELP FEELING...

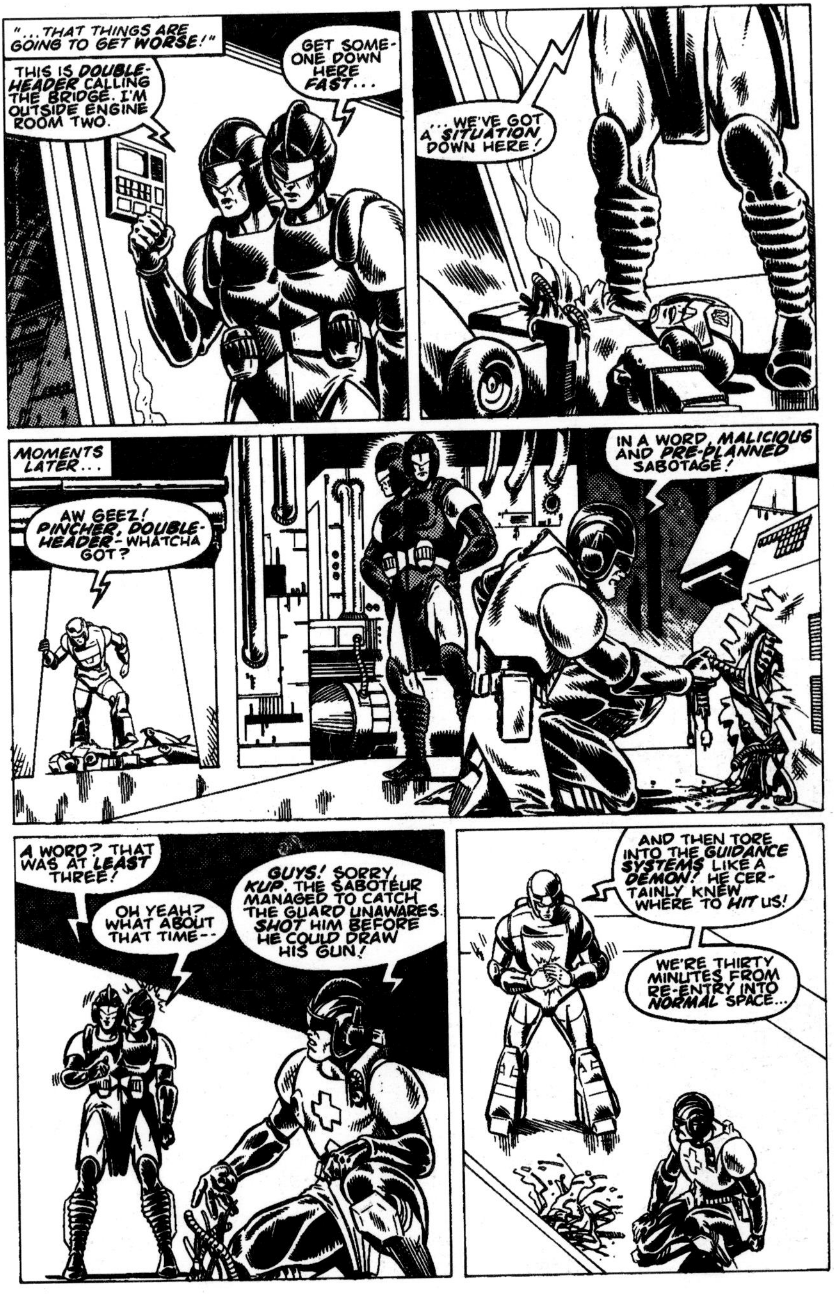
"...THAT THINGS ARE GOING TO GET WORSE!"
THIS IS DOUBLE-HEADER CALLING THE BRIDGE. I'M OUTSIDE ENGINE ROOM TWO.
GET SOME-ONE DOWN HERE FAST...
...WE'VE GOT A SITUATION DOWN HERE!
MOMENTS LATER...
AW GEEZ! PINCHER, DOUBLE-HEADER--WHATCHA GOT?
IN A WORD, MALICIOUS AND PRE-PLANNED SABOTAGE!
A WORD? THAT WAS AT LEAST THREE!
OH YEAH? WHAT ABOUT THAT TIME--
GUYS! SORRY, KUP. THE SABOTEUR MANAGED TO CATCH THE GUARD UNAWARES. SHOT HIM BEFORE HE COULD DRAW HIS GUN!
AND THEN TORE INTO THE GUIDANCE SYSTEMS LIKE A DEMON! HE CERTAINLY KNEW WHERE TO HIT US!
WE'RE THIRTY MINUTES FROM RE-ENTRY INTO NORMAL SPACE...

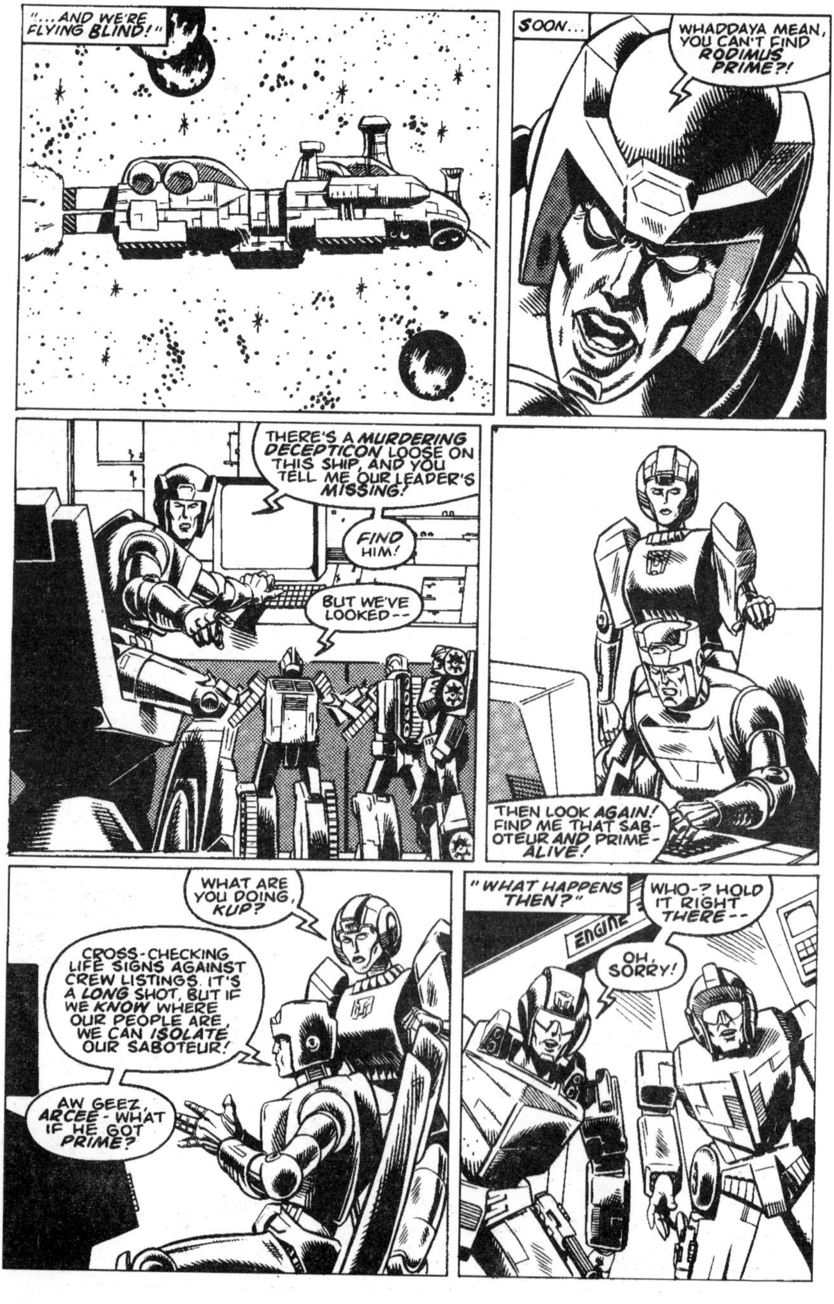
"...AND WE'RE FLYING BLIND!"
SOON...
WHADDAYA MEAN, YOU CAN'T FIND RODIMUS PRIME?!
THERE'S A MURDERING DECEPTICON LOOSE ON THIS SHIP, AND YOU TELL ME OUR LEADER'S MISSING!
FIND HIM!
BUT WE'VE LOOKED--
THEN LOOK AGAIN! FIND ME THAT SABOTEUR AND PRIME-ALIVE!
WHAT ARE YOU DOING, KUP?
CROSS-CHECKING LIFE SIGNS AGAINST CREW LISTINGS. IT'S A LONG SHOT, BUT IF WE KNOW WHERE OUR PEOPLE ARE, WE CAN ISOLATE OUR SABOTEUR!
AW GEEZ, ARCEE- WHAT IF HE GOT PRIME?
"WHAT HAPPENS THEN?"
WHO-? HOLD IT RIGHT THERE--
ENGINE
OH, SORRY!

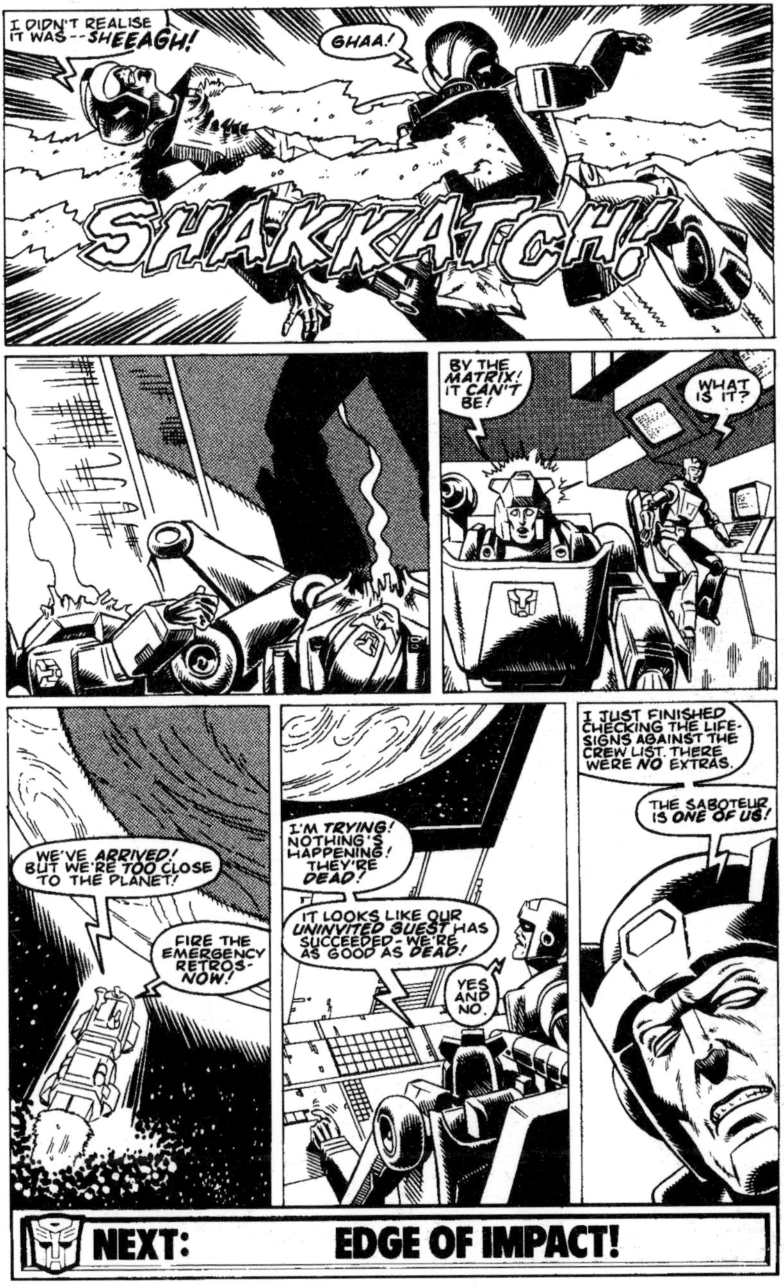
I DIDN'T REALISE IT WAS--SHEEAGH!
GHAA!
SHAKKATCH!
BY THE MATRIX! IT CAN'T BE!
WHAT IS IT?
WE'VE ARRIVED! BUT WE'RE TOO CLOSE TO THE PLANET!
FIRE THE EMERGENCY RETROS-NOW!
I'M TRYING! NOTHING'S HAPPENING! THEY'RE DEAD!
IT LOOKS LIKE OUR UNINVITED GUEST HAS SUCCEEDED- WE'RE AS GOOD AS DEAD!
YES AND NO.
I JUST FINISHED CHECKING THE LIFE-SIGNS AGAINST THE CREW LIST. THERE WERE NO EXTRAS.
THE SABOTEUR IS ONE OF US!

NEXT: EDGE OF IMPACT!

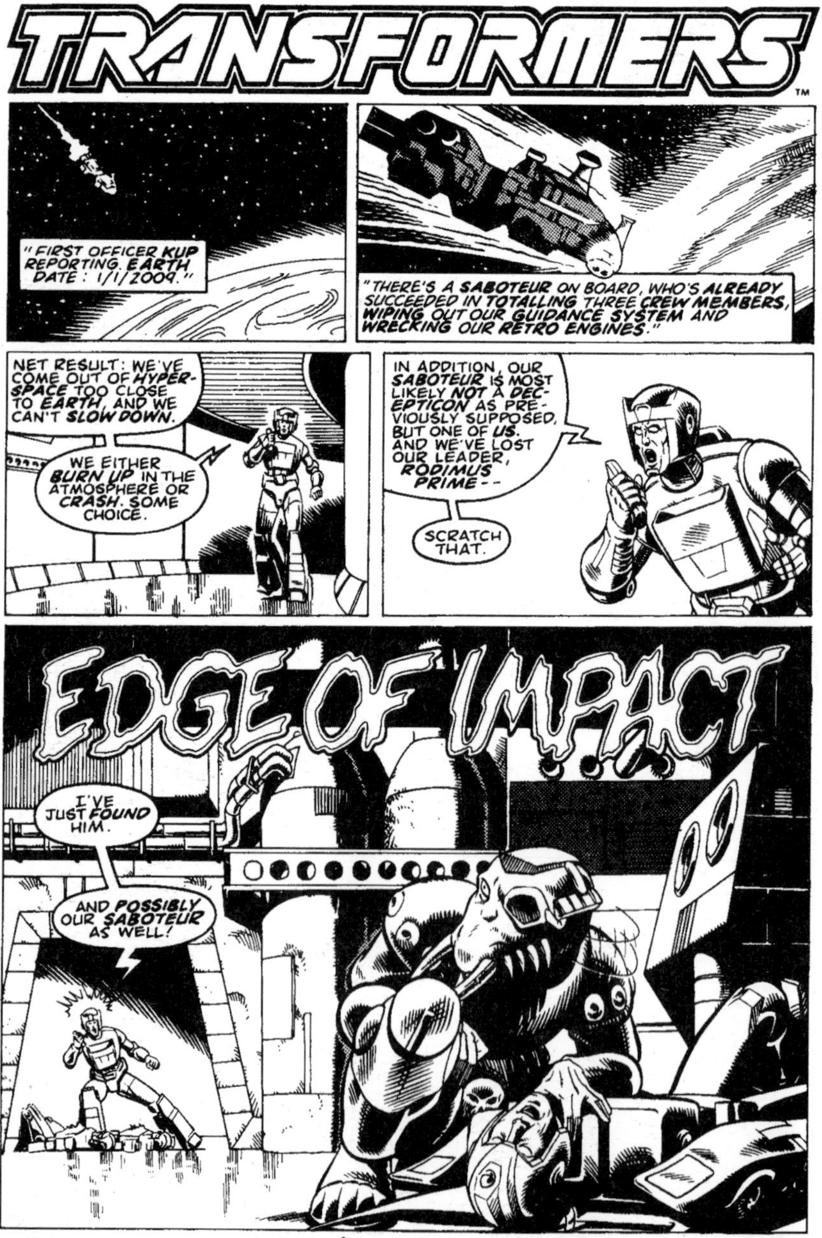
TRANSFORMERS
"FIRST OFFICER KUP REPORTING. EARTH DATE: 1/1/2009."
"THERE'S A SABOTEUR ON BOARD, WHO'S ALREADY SUCCEEDED IN TOTALLING THREE CREW MEMBERS, WIPING OUT OUR GUIDANCE SYSTEM AND WRECKING OUR RETRO ENGINES."
NET RESULT: WE'VE COME OUT OF HYPER-SPACE TOO CLOSE TO EARTH, AND WE CAN'T SLOW DOWN.
WE EITHER BURN UP IN THE ATMOSPHERE OR CRASH. SOME CHOICE.
IN ADDITION, OUR SABOTEUR IS MOST LIKELY NOT A DECEPTICON AS PREVIOUSLY SUPPOSED, BUT ONE OF US. AND WE'VE LOST OUR LEADER, RODIMUS PRIME--
SCRATCH THAT.
EDGE OF IMPACT
I'VE JUST FOUND HIM.
AND POSSIBLY OUR SABOTEUR AS WELL!

Script Simon Furman **Art** Staz **Letters** Glib

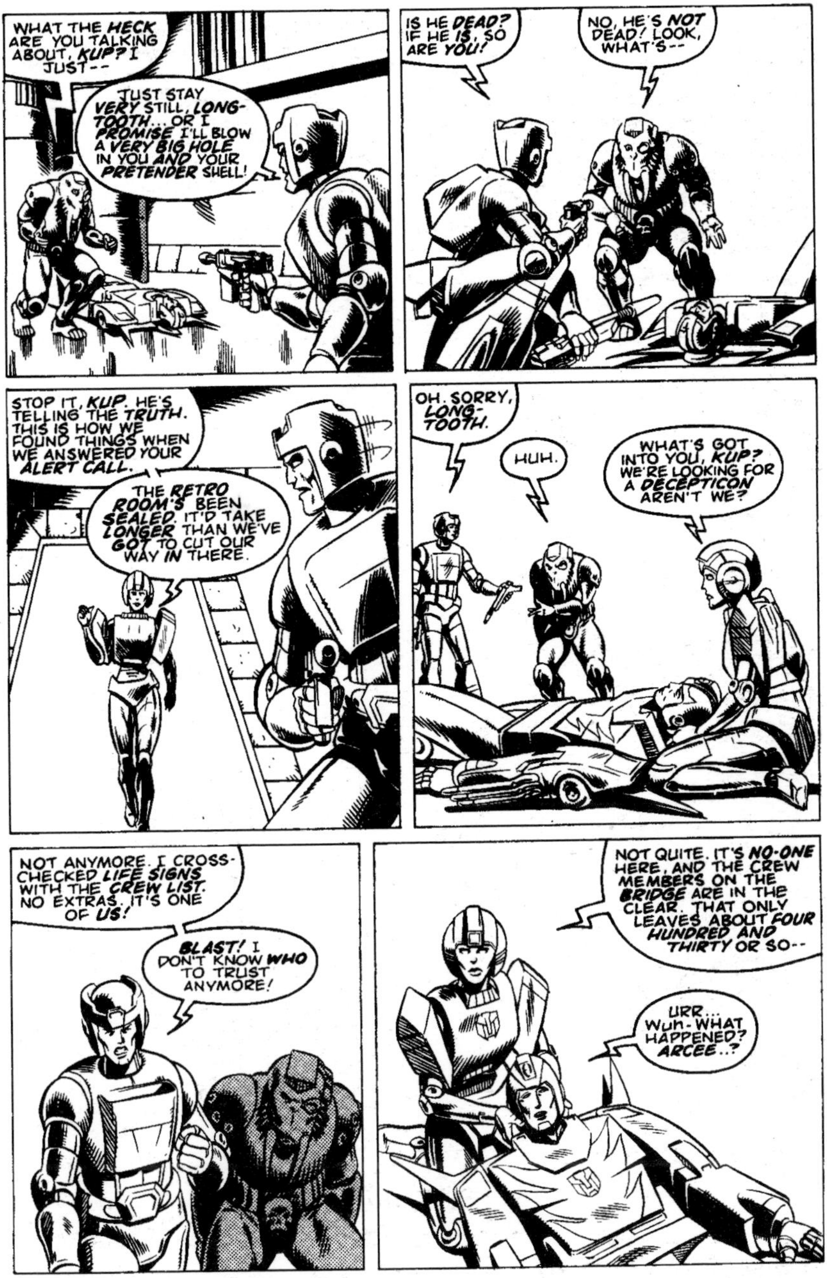
WHAT THE HECK ARE YOU TALKING ABOUT, KUP? I JUST--
JUST STAY VERY STILL, LONG-TOOTH... OR I PROMISE I'LL BLOW A VERY BIG HOLE IN YOU AND YOUR PRETENDER SHELL!
IS HE DEAD? IF HE IS, SO ARE YOU!
NO, HE'S NOT DEAD! LOOK, WHAT'S--
STOP IT, KUP. HE'S TELLING THE TRUTH. THIS IS HOW WE FOUND THINGS WHEN WE ANSWERED YOUR ALERT CALL.
THE RETRO ROOM'S BEEN SEALED. IT'D TAKE LONGER THAN WE'VE GOT TO CUT OUR WAY IN THERE.
OH. SORRY, LONG-TOOTH.
HUH.
WHAT'S GOT INTO YOU, KUP? WE'RE LOOKING FOR A DECEPTICON AREN'T WE?
NOT ANYMORE. I CROSS-CHECKED LIFE SIGNS WITH THE CREW LIST. NO EXTRAS. IT'S ONE OF US!
BLAST! I DON'T KNOW WHO TO TRUST ANYMORE!
NOT QUITE. IT'S NO-ONE HERE, AND THE CREW MEMBERS ON THE BRIDGE ARE IN THE CLEAR. THAT ONLY LEAVES ABOUT FOUR HUNDRED AND THIRTY OR SO--
URR... WUH-WHAT HAPPENED? ARCEE..?

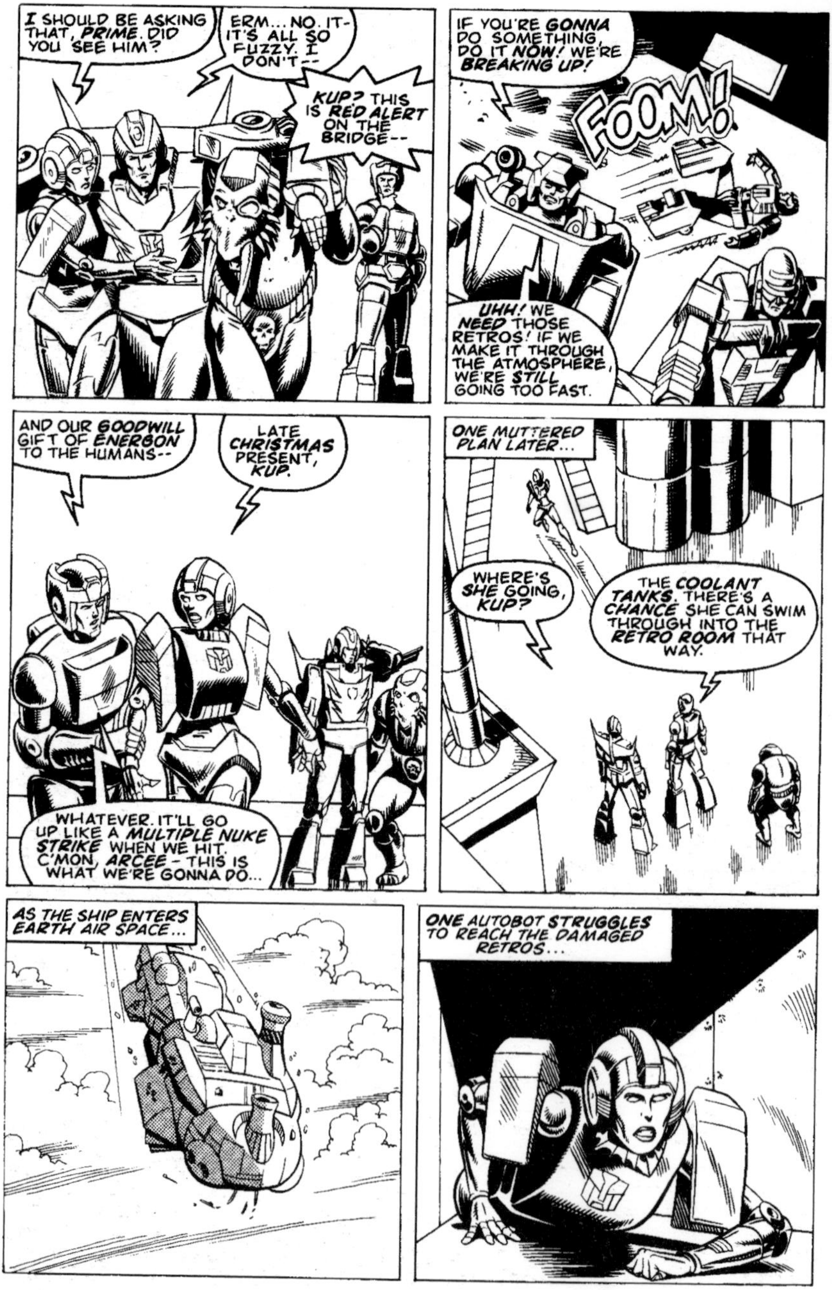
I SHOULD BE ASKING THAT, PRIME. DID YOU SEE HIM?
ERM... NO. IT-IT'S ALL SO FUZZY. I DON'T--
KUP? THIS IS RED ALERT ON THE BRIDGE--
IF YOU'RE GONNA DO SOMETHING, DO IT NOW! WE'RE BREAKING UP!
FOOM!
UHH! WE NEED THOSE RETROS! IF WE MAKE IT THROUGH THE ATMOSPHERE, WE'RE STILL GOING TOO FAST.
AND OUR GOODWILL GIFT OF ENERGON TO THE HUMANS--
LATE CHRISTMAS PRESENT, KUP.
WHATEVER. IT'LL GO UP LIKE A MULTIPLE NUKE STRIKE WHEN WE HIT. C'MON, ARCEE - THIS IS WHAT WE'RE GONNA DO...
ONE MUTTERED PLAN LATER...
WHERE'S SHE GOING, KUP?
THE COOLANT TANKS. THERE'S A CHANCE SHE CAN SWIM THROUGH INTO THE RETRO ROOM THAT WAY.
AS THE SHIP ENTERS EARTH AIR SPACE...
ONE AUTOBOT STRUGGLES TO REACH THE DAMAGED RETROS...

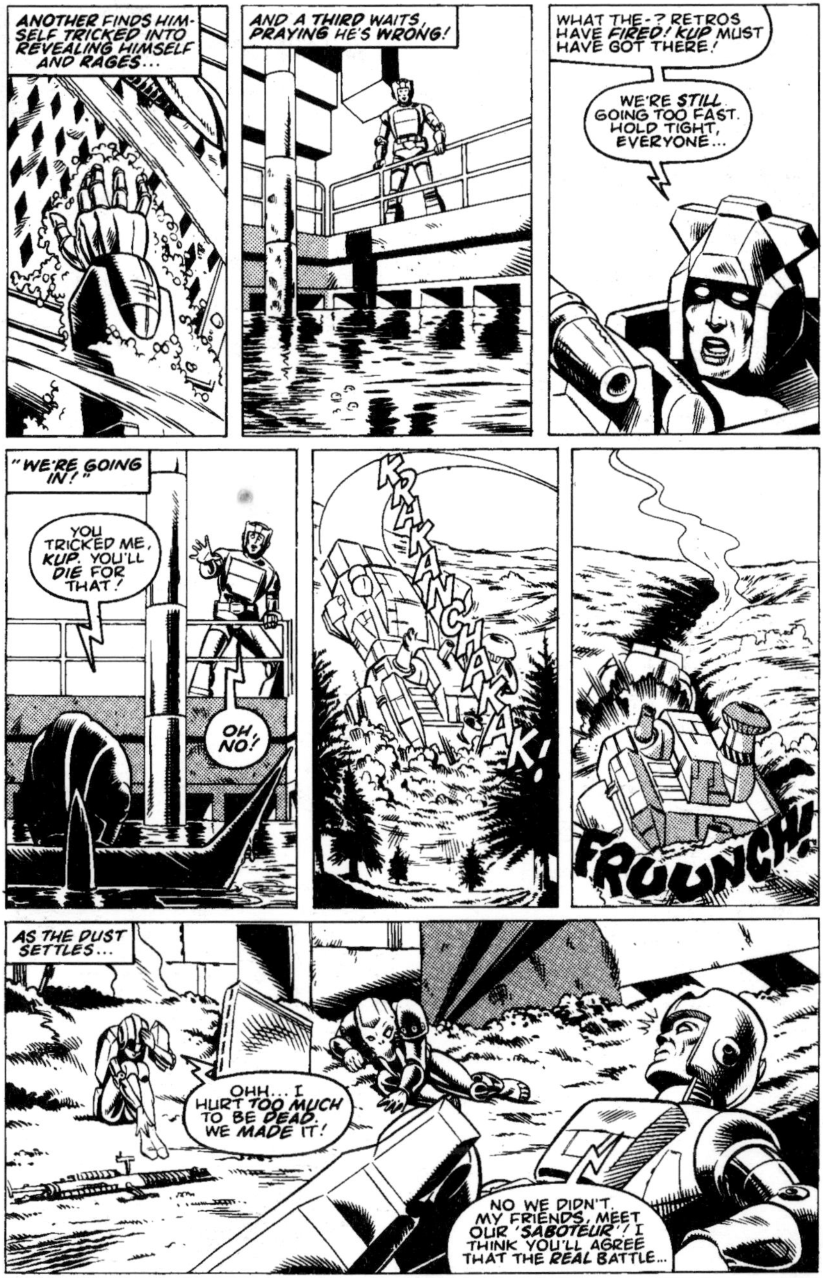
ANOTHER FINDS HIMSELF TRICKED INTO REVEALING HIMSELF AND RAGES...
AND A THIRD WAITS, PRAYING HE'S WRONG!
WHAT THE-? RETROS HAVE FIRED! KUP MUST HAVE GOT THERE!
WE'RE STILL GOING TOO FAST. HOLD TIGHT, EVERYONE...
"WE'RE GOING IN!"
YOU TRICKED ME, KUP. YOU'LL DIE FOR THAT!
OH, NO!
KRAKANCHAKAK!
FRUUNCH!
AS THE DUST SETTLES...
OHH... I HURT TOO MUCH TO BE DEAD. WE MADE IT!
NO WE DIDN'T. MY FRIENDS, MEET OUR 'SABOTEUR'! I THINK YOU'LL AGREE THAT THE REAL BATTLE...

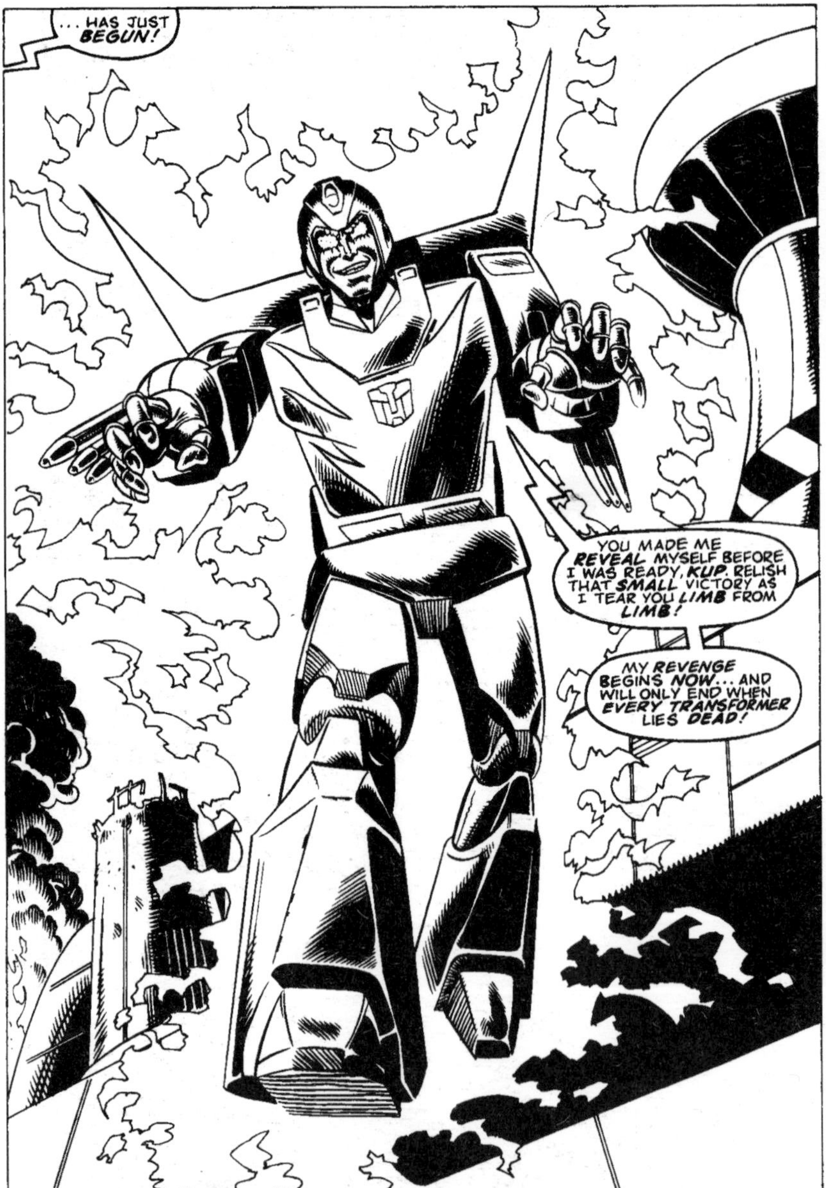
... HAS JUST BEGUN!
YOU MADE ME REVEAL MYSELF BEFORE I WAS READY, KUP. RELISH THAT SMALL VICTORY AS I TEAR YOU LIMB FROM LIMB!
MY REVENGE BEGINS NOW... AND WILL ONLY END WHEN EVERY TRANSFORMER LIES DEAD!

NEXT: GENOCIDE!

TRANSFORMERS™

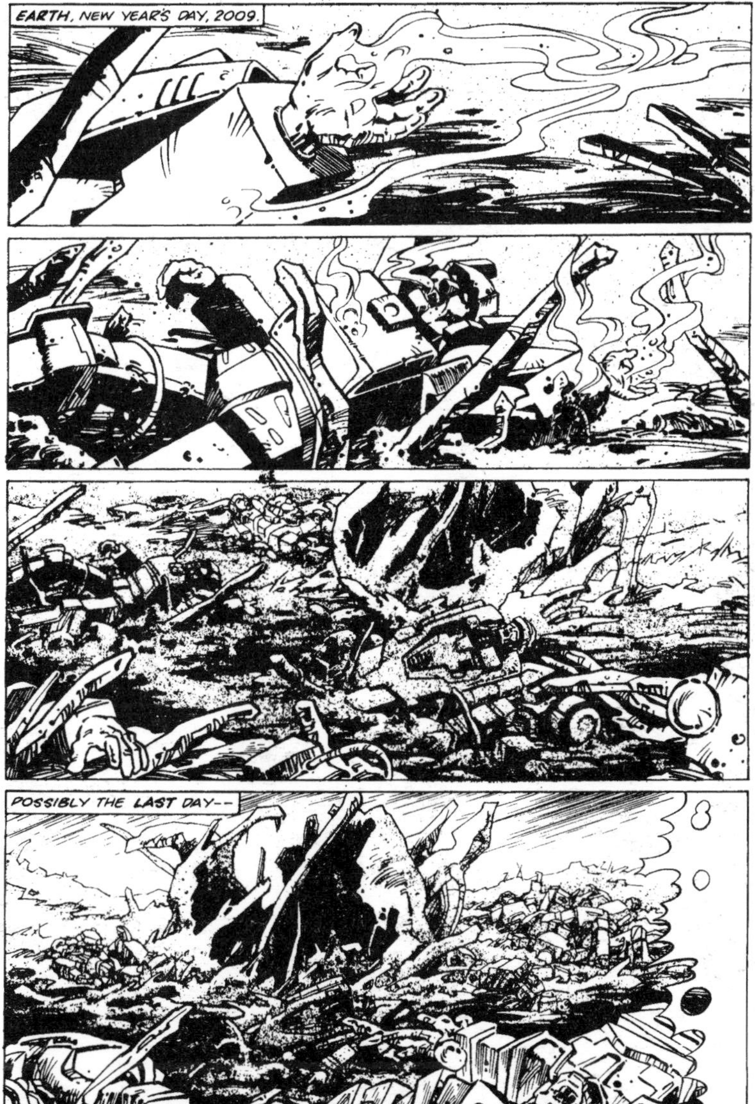
EARTH, NEW YEAR'S DAY, 2009.
POSSIBLY THE LAST DAY--

Script Simon Furman **Art** Cam S **Letters** Annie Halfacree

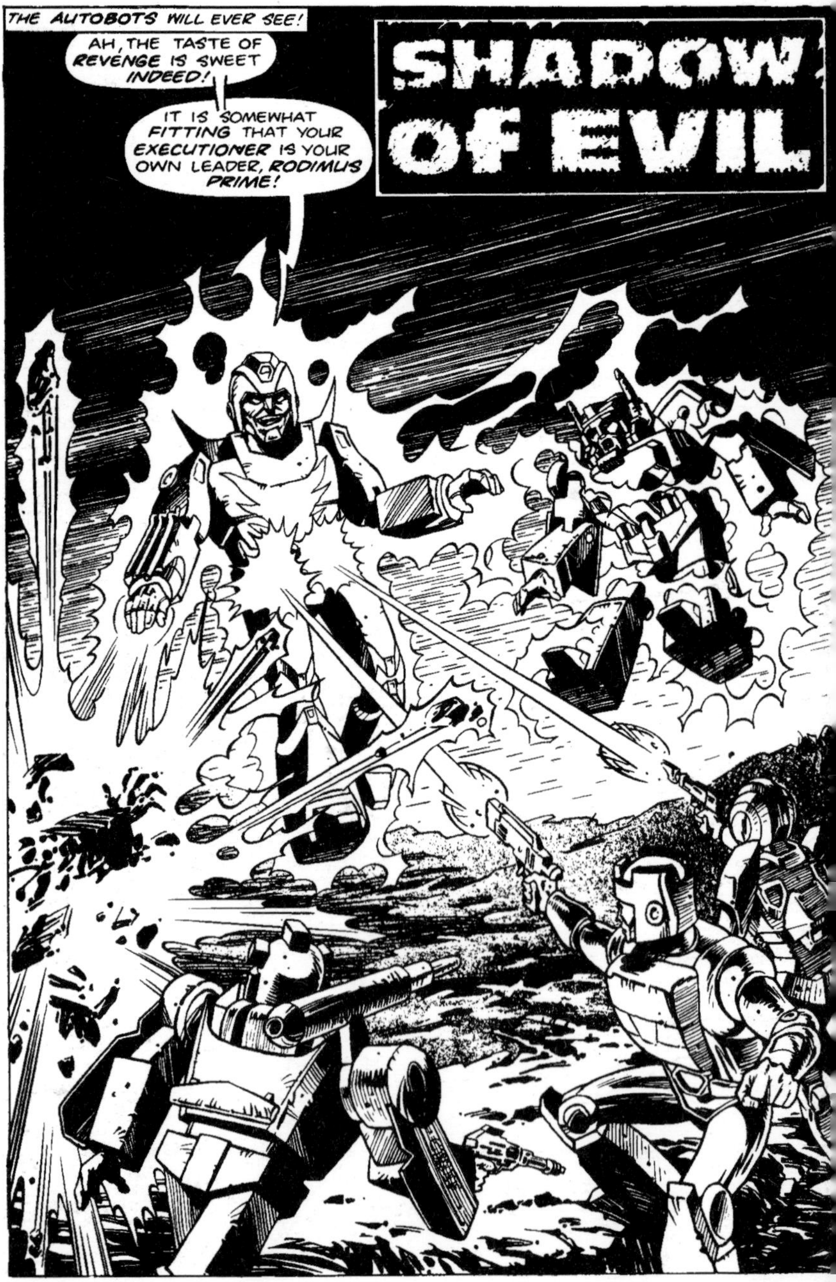
THE AUTOBOTS WILL EVER SEE!
AH, THE TASTE OF REVENGE IS SWEET INDEED!
IT IS SOMEWHAT FITTING THAT YOUR EXECUTIONER IS YOUR OWN LEADER, RODIMUS PRIME!
SHADOW OF EVIL

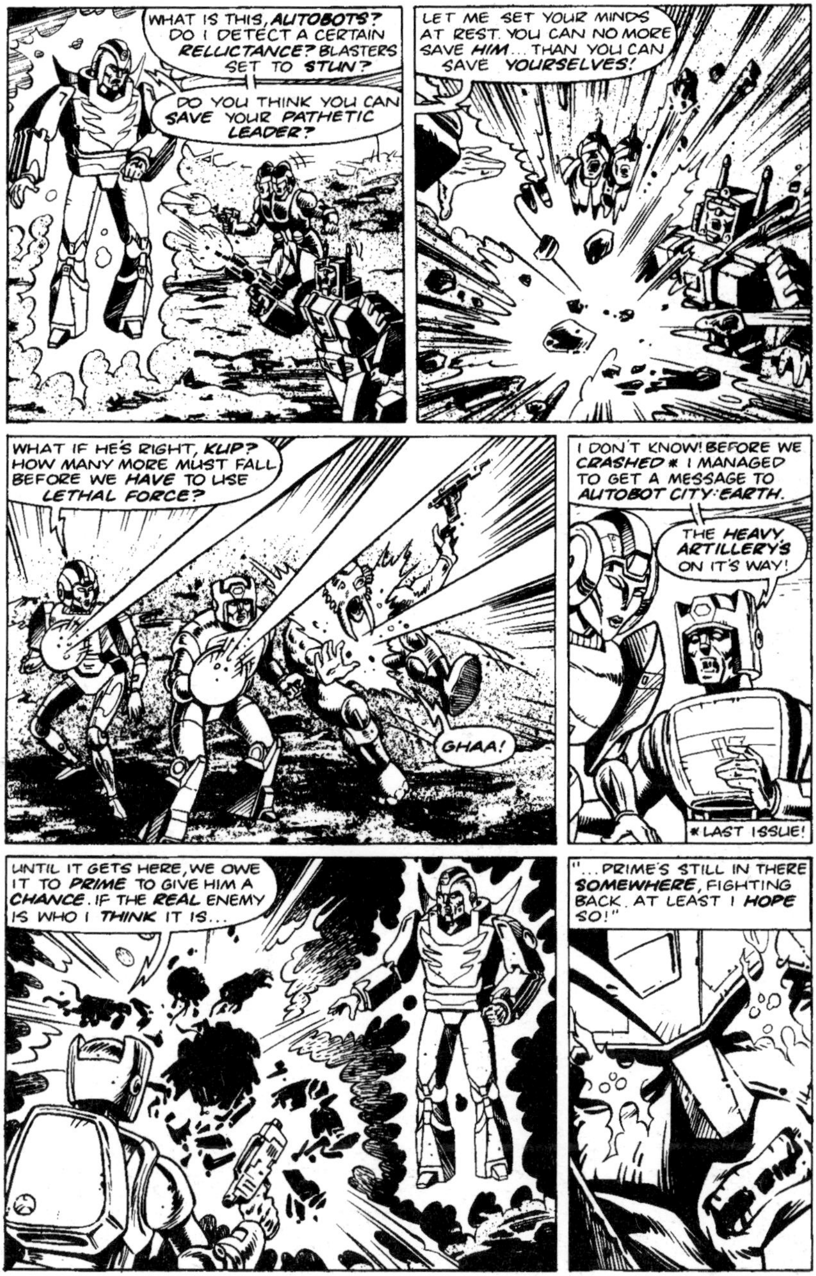
WHAT IS THIS, AUTOBOTS? DO I DETECT A CERTAIN RELUCTANCE? BLASTERS SET TO STUN?
DO YOU THINK YOU CAN SAVE YOUR PATHETIC LEADER?
LET ME SET YOUR MINDS AT REST. YOU CAN NO MORE SAVE HIM... THAN YOU CAN SAVE YOURSELVES!
WHAT IF HE'S RIGHT, KUP? HOW MANY MORE MUST FALL BEFORE WE HAVE TO USE LETHAL FORCE?
GHAA!
I DON'T KNOW! BEFORE WE CRASHED * I MANAGED TO GET A MESSAGE TO AUTOBOT CITY: EARTH.
THE HEAVY ARTILLERY'S ON IT'S WAY!
* LAST ISSUE!
UNTIL IT GETS HERE, WE OWE IT TO PRIME TO GIVE HIM A CHANCE. IF THE REAL ENEMY IS WHO I THINK IT IS...
"...PRIME'S STILL IN THERE SOMEWHERE, FIGHTING BACK. AT LEAST I HOPE SO!"

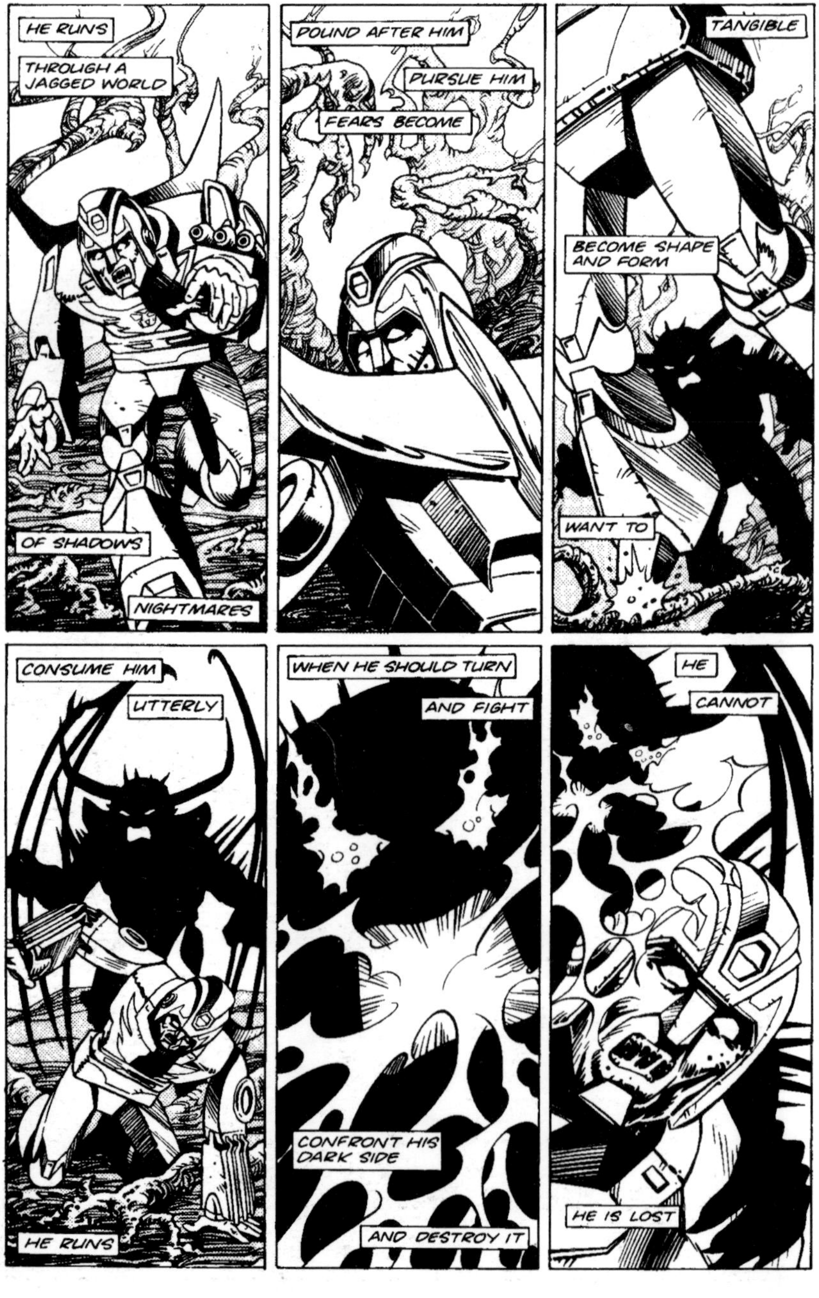
HE RUNS
THROUGH A JAGGED WORLD
OF SHADOWS
NIGHTMARES
POUND AFTER HIM
PURSUE HIM
FEARS BECOME
TANGIBLE
BECOME SHAPE AND FORM
WANT TO
CONSUME HIM
UTTERLY
HE RUNS
WHEN HE SHOULD TURN
AND FIGHT
CONFRONT HIS DARK SIDE
AND DESTROY IT
HE
CANNOT
HE IS LOST

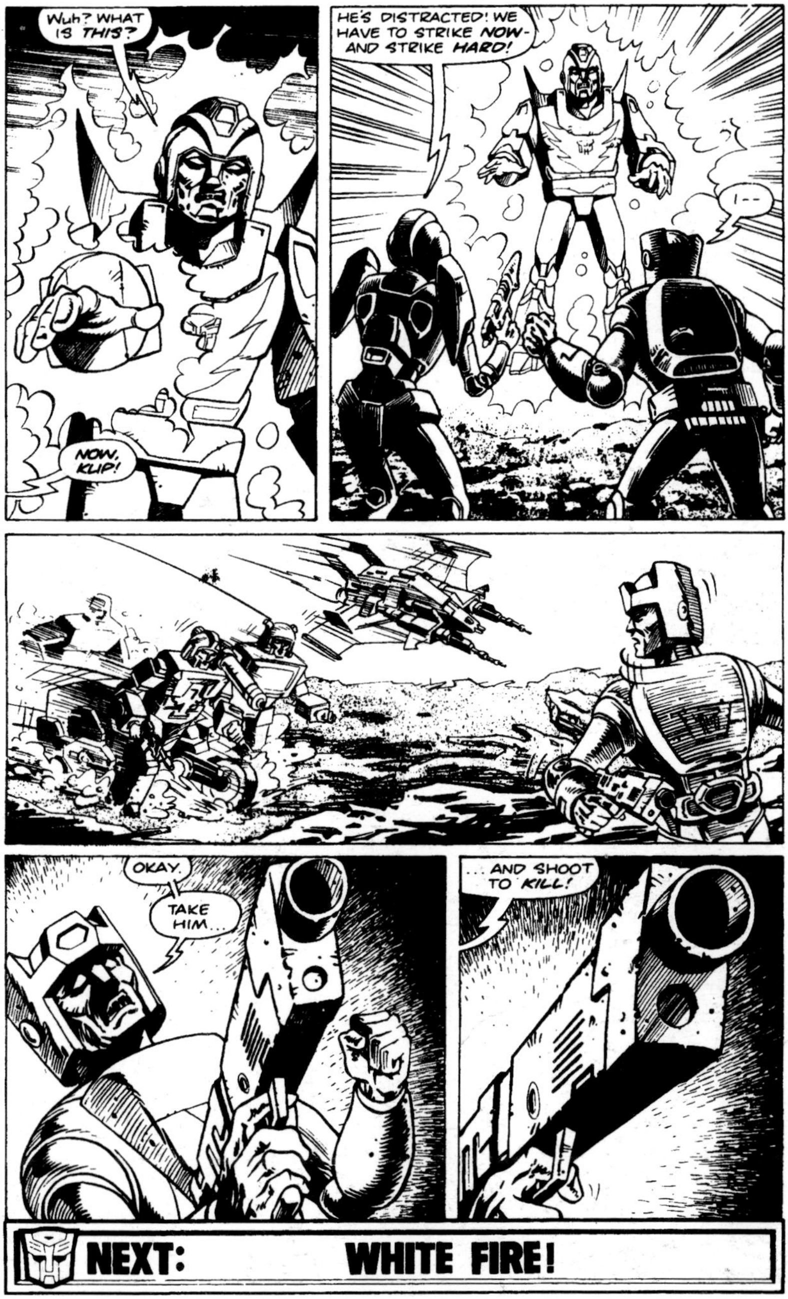
Wuh? WHAT IS THIS?
NOW, KLIP!
HE'S DISTRACTED! WE HAVE TO STRIKE NOW- AND STRIKE HARD!
I--
OKAY.
TAKE HIM...
...AND SHOOT TO KILL!
NEXT: WHITE FIRE!

TRANSFORMERS™

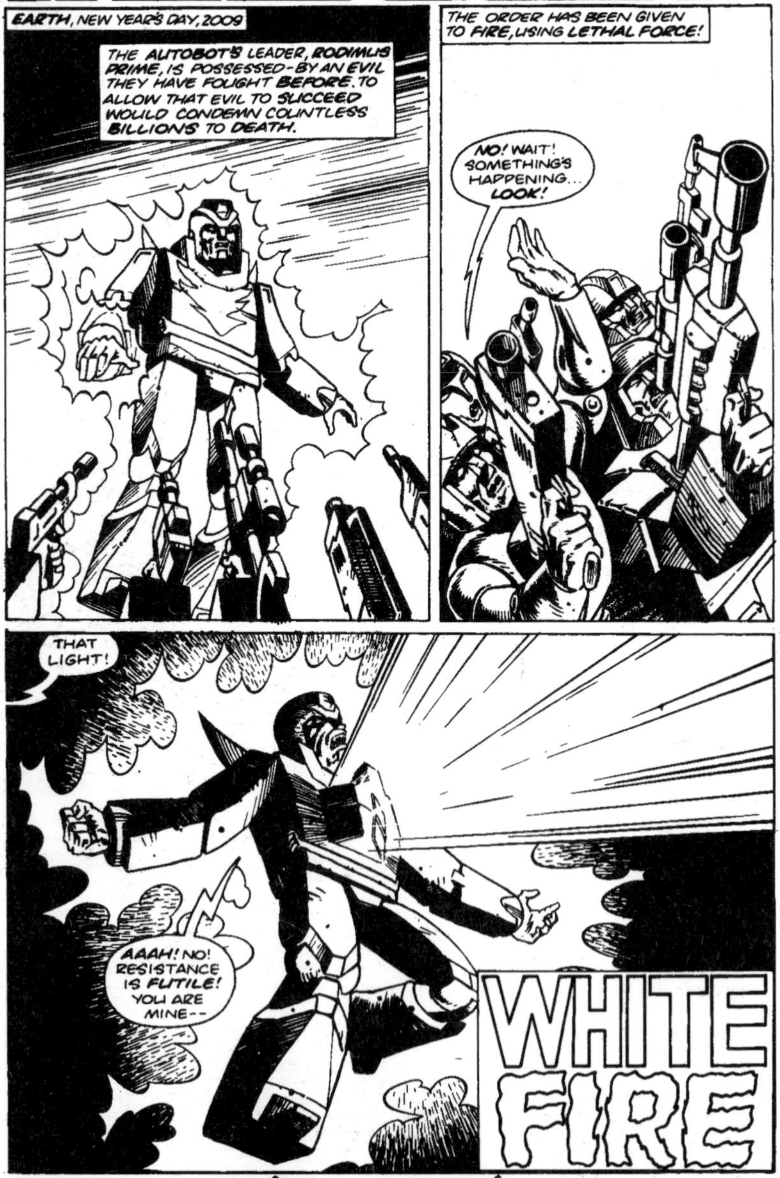
EARTH, NEW YEAR'S DAY, 2009
THE AUTOBOT'S LEADER, RODIMUS PRIME, IS POSSESSED--BY AN EVIL THEY HAVE FOUGHT BEFORE. TO ALLOW THAT EVIL TO SUCCEED WOULD CONDEMN COUNTLESS BILLIONS TO DEATH.
THE ORDER HAS BEEN GIVEN TO FIRE, USING LETHAL FORCE!
NO! WAIT! SOMETHING'S HAPPENING... LOOK!
THAT LIGHT!
AAAH! NO! RESISTANCE IS FUTILE! YOU ARE MINE--
WHITE FIRE

Script Simon Furman · Art Cam Smith · Letters Stuart Bartlett

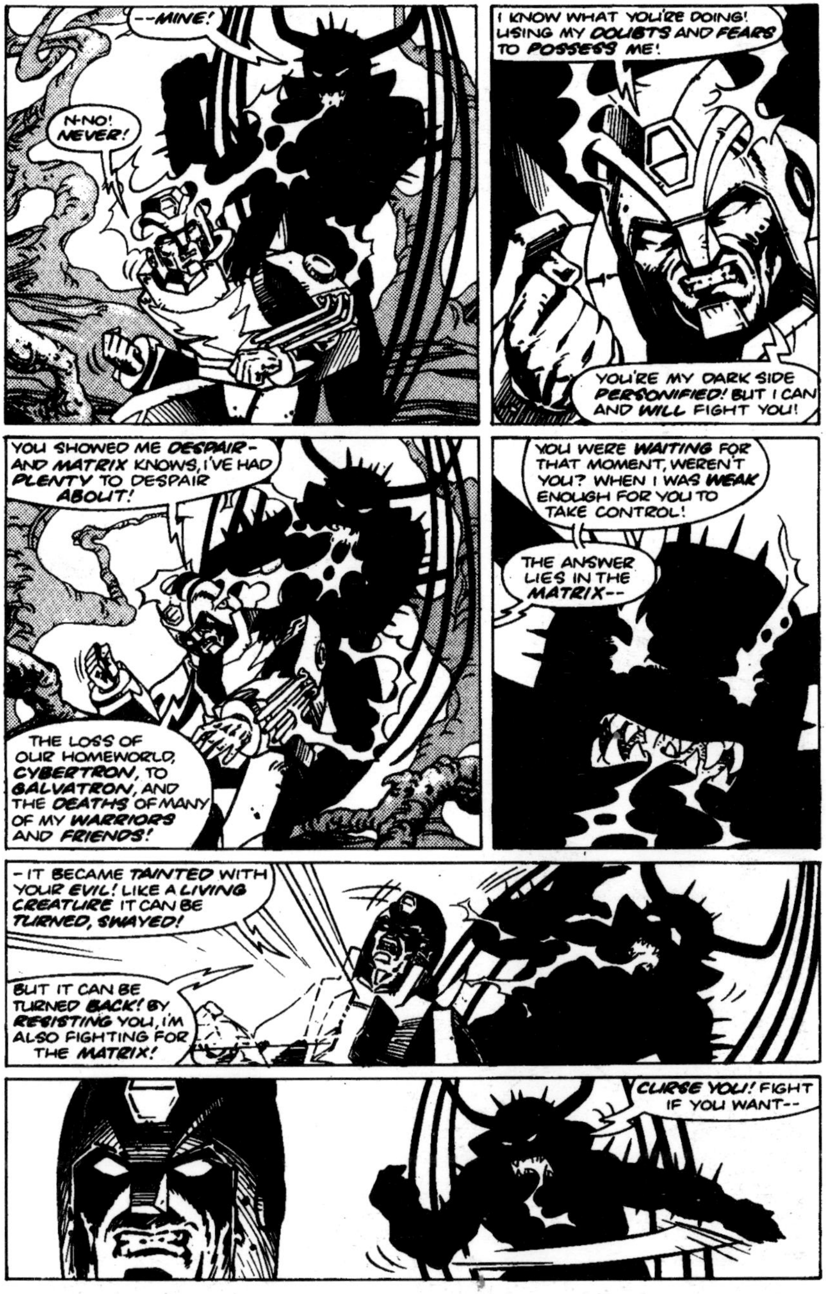
--MINE!
N-NO! NEVER!
I KNOW WHAT YOU'RE DOING! USING MY DOUBTS AND FEARS TO POSSESS ME!
YOU'RE MY DARK SIDE PERSONIFIED! BUT I CAN AND WILL FIGHT YOU!
YOU SHOWED ME DESPAIR-- AND MATRIX KNOWS, I'VE HAD PLENTY TO DESPAIR ABOUT!
THE LOSS OF OUR HOMEWORLD, CYBERTRON, TO GALVATRON, AND THE DEATHS OF MANY OF MY WARRIORS AND FRIENDS!
YOU WERE WAITING FOR THAT MOMENT, WEREN'T YOU? WHEN I WAS WEAK ENOUGH FOR YOU TO TAKE CONTROL!
THE ANSWER LIES IN THE MATRIX--
-IT BECAME TAINTED WITH YOUR EVIL! LIKE A LIVING CREATURE IT CAN BE TURNED, SWAYED!
BUT IT CAN BE TURNED BACK! BY RESISTING YOU, I'M ALSO FIGHTING FOR THE MATRIX!
CURSE YOU! FIGHT IF YOU WANT--

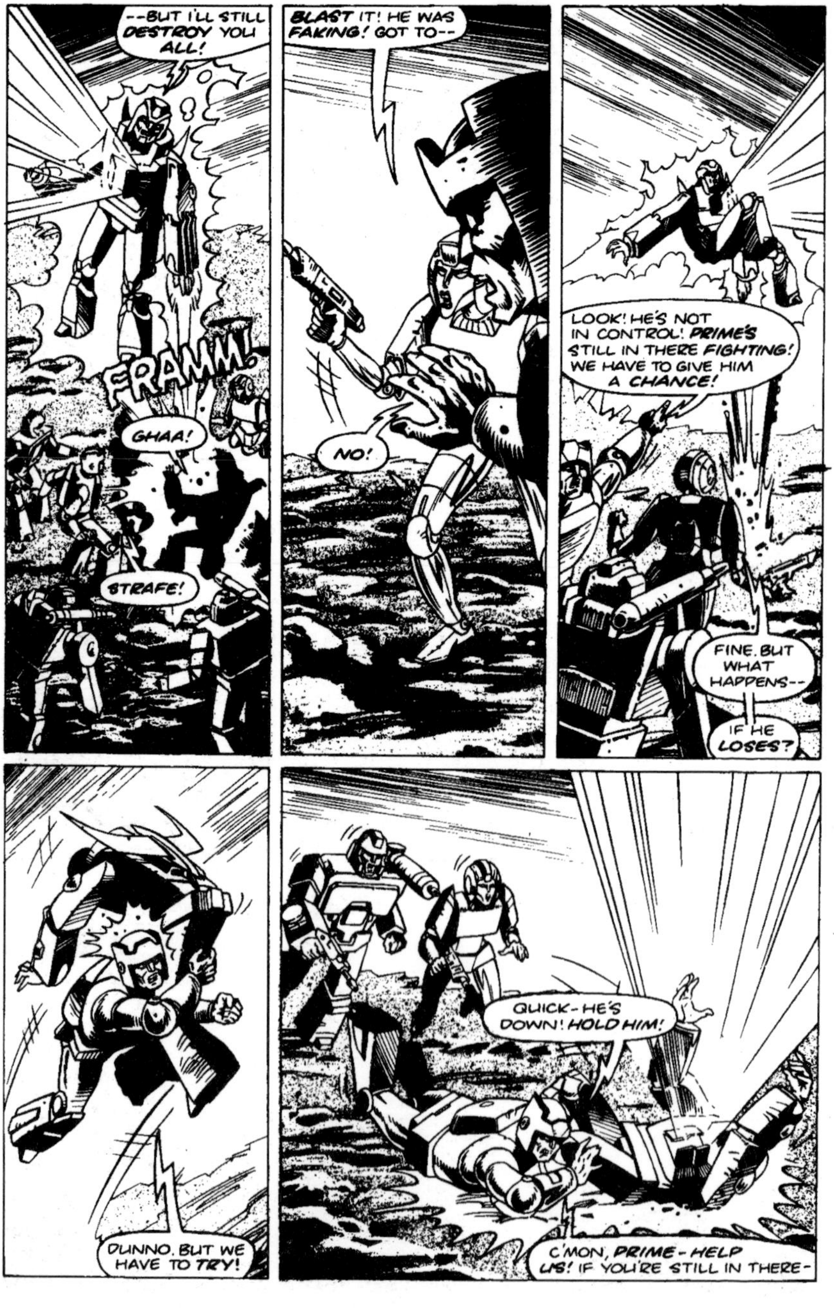
--BUT I'LL STILL DESTROY YOU ALL!
FRAMM!
GHAA!
STRAFE!
BLAST IT! HE WAS FAKING! GOT TO--
NO!
LOOK! HE'S NOT IN CONTROL! PRIME'S STILL IN THERE FIGHTING! WE HAVE TO GIVE HIM A CHANCE!
FINE. BUT WHAT HAPPENS--
IF HE LOSES?
DUNNO. BUT WE HAVE TO TRY!
QUICK - HE'S DOWN! HOLD HIM!
C'MON, PRIME - HELP US! IF YOU'RE STILL IN THERE-

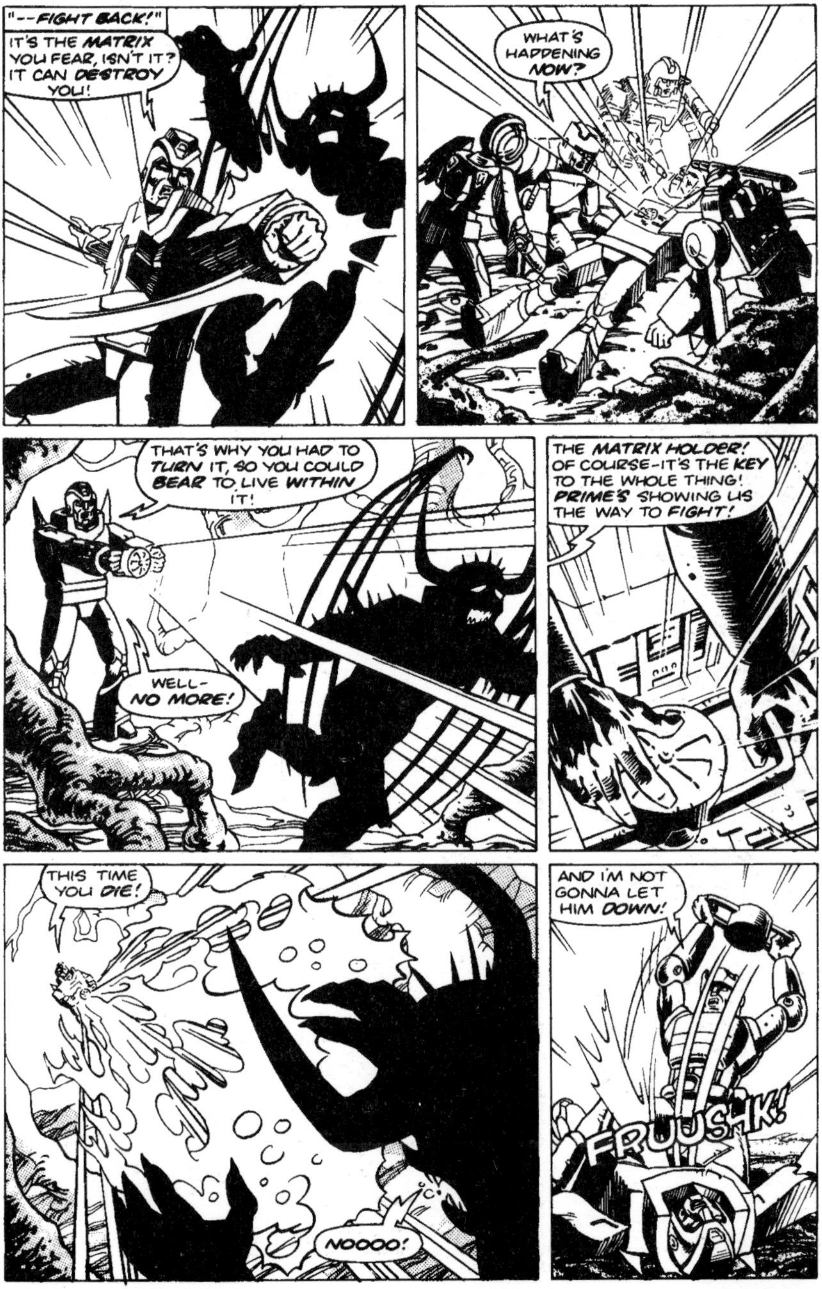
"--FIGHT BACK!"
IT'S THE MATRIX YOU FEAR, ISN'T IT? IT CAN DESTROY YOU!
WHAT'S HAPPENING NOW?
THAT'S WHY YOU HAD TO TURN IT, SO YOU COULD BEAR TO LIVE WITHIN IT!
WELL- NO MORE!
THE MATRIX HOLDER! OF COURSE-IT'S THE KEY TO THE WHOLE THING! PRIME'S SHOWING US THE WAY TO FIGHT!
THIS TIME YOU DIE!
NOOOO!
AND I'M NOT GONNA LET HIM DOWN!
FRUUSHK!

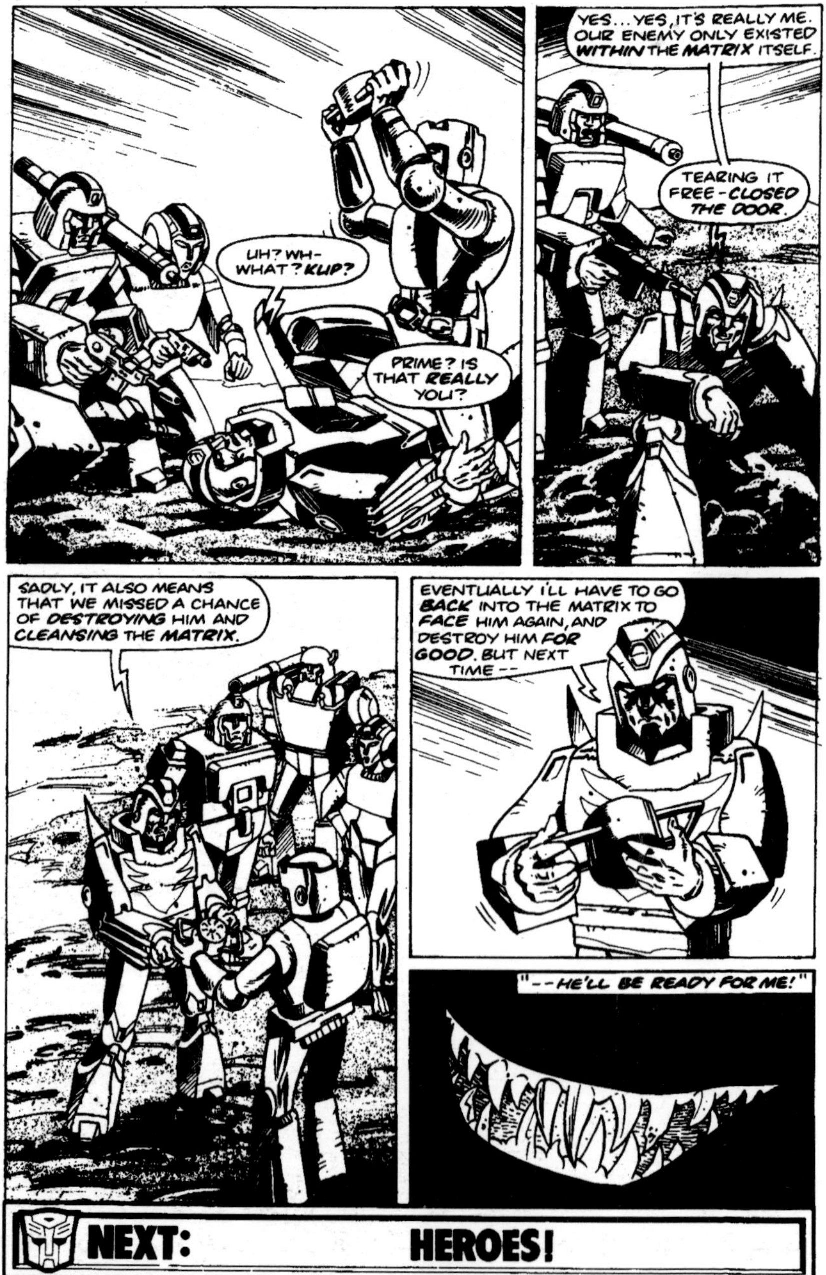
UH? WH- WHAT? KUP?
PRIME? IS THAT REALLY YOU?
YES... YES, IT'S REALLY ME. OUR ENEMY ONLY EXISTED WITHIN THE MATRIX ITSELF.
TEARING IT FREE - CLOSED THE DOOR.
SADLY, IT ALSO MEANS THAT WE MISSED A CHANCE OF DESTROYING HIM AND CLEANSING THE MATRIX.
EVENTUALLY I'LL HAVE TO GO BACK INTO THE MATRIX TO FACE HIM AGAIN, AND DESTROY HIM FOR GOOD. BUT NEXT TIME --
"--HE'LL BE READY FOR ME!"
NEXT: HEROES!

TRANSFORMERS™

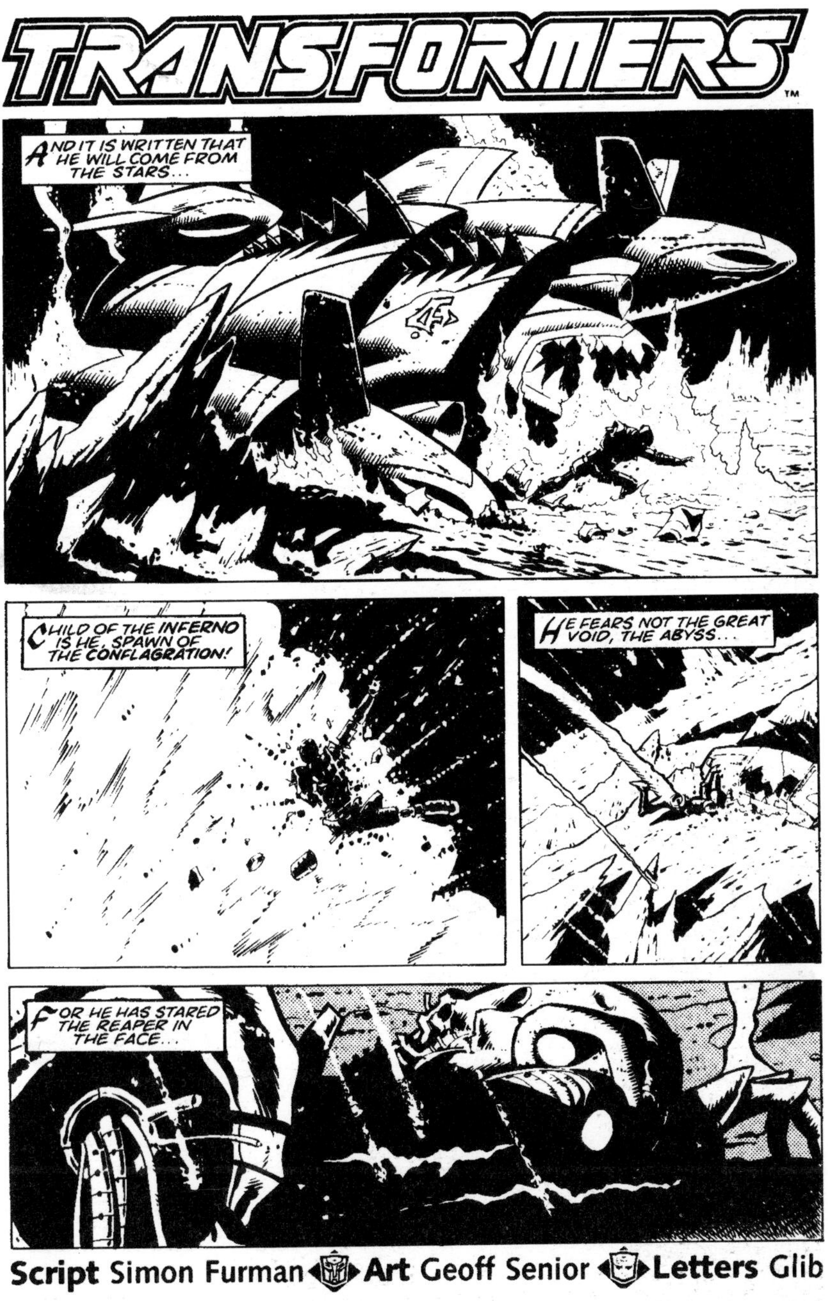
AND IT IS WRITTEN THAT HE WILL COME FROM THE STARS...
CHILD OF THE INFERNO IS HE, SPAWN OF THE CONFLAGRATION!
HE FEARS NOT THE GREAT VOID, THE ABYSS...
FOR HE HAS STARED THE REAPER IN THE FACE...

Script Simon Furman **Art** Geoff Senior **Letters** Glib

AND HIS EYES HAVE SEEN THE GLORY!

THE POWER TO CREATE OR DESTROY IS HIS TO WIELD...

LET HIS NAME AND PURPOSE BE FORGED AS ONE!

SAY HIS NAME! CRY...

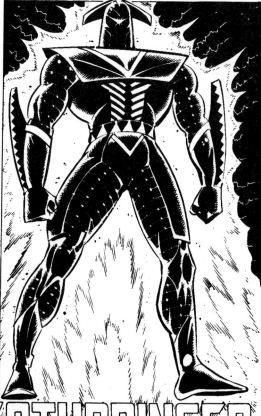

DEATHBRINGER

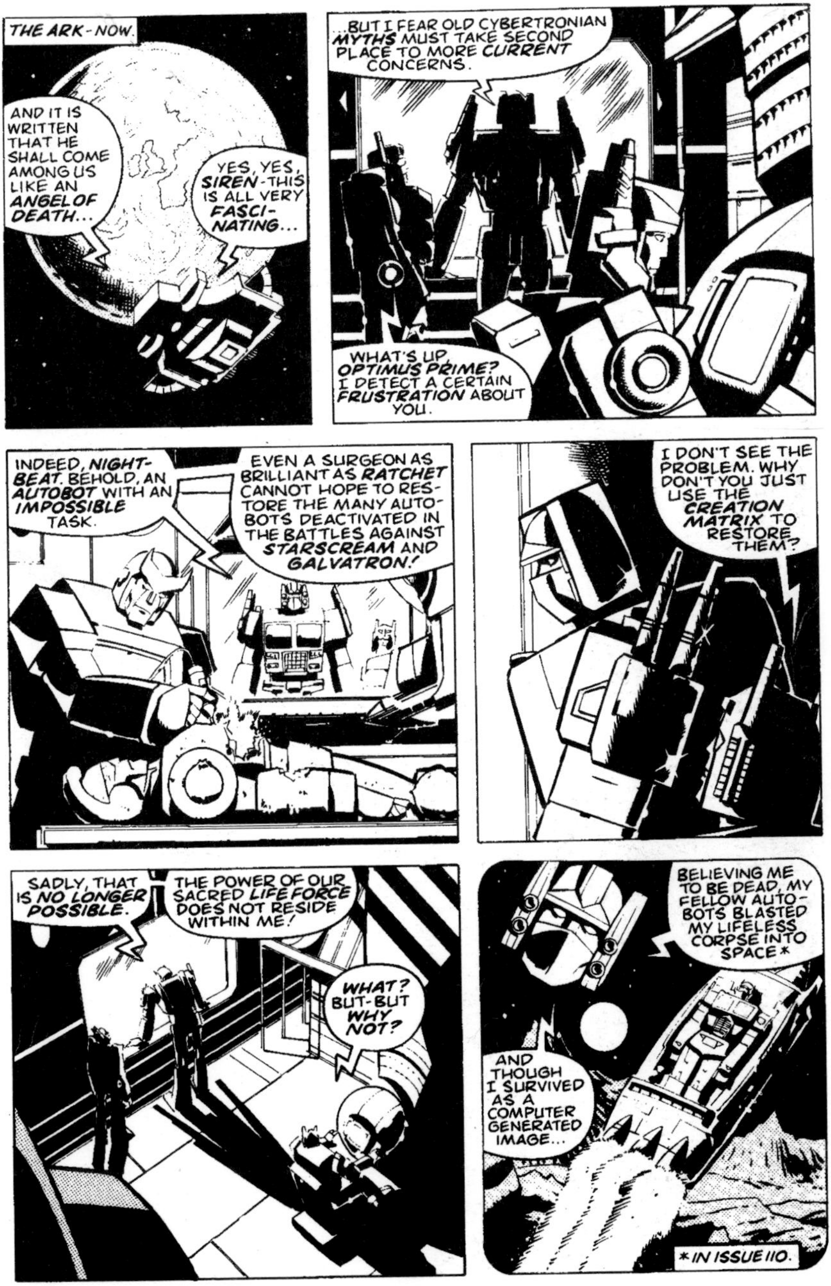
THE ARK - NOW.
AND IT IS WRITTEN THAT HE SHALL COME AMONG US LIKE AN ANGEL OF DEATH...
YES, YES, SIREN - THIS IS ALL VERY FASCINATING...
...BUT I FEAR OLD CYBERTRONIAN MYTHS MUST TAKE SECOND PLACE TO MORE CURRENT CONCERNS.
WHAT'S UP OPTIMUS PRIME? I DETECT A CERTAIN FRUSTRATION ABOUT YOU.
INDEED, NIGHTBEAT. BEHOLD, AN AUTOBOT WITH AN IMPOSSIBLE TASK.
EVEN A SURGEON AS BRILLIANT AS RATCHET CANNOT HOPE TO RESTORE THE MANY AUTOBOTS DEACTIVATED IN THE BATTLES AGAINST STARSCREAM AND GALVATRON!
I DON'T SEE THE PROBLEM. WHY DON'T YOU JUST USE THE CREATION MATRIX TO RESTORE THEM?
SADLY, THAT IS NO LONGER POSSIBLE.
THE POWER OF OUR SACRED LIFE FORCE DOES NOT RESIDE WITHIN ME!
WHAT? BUT-BUT WHY NOT?
BELIEVING ME TO BE DEAD, MY FELLOW AUTOBOTS BLASTED MY LIFELESS CORPSE INTO SPACE *
AND THOUGH I SURVIVED AS A COMPUTER GENERATED IMAGE...
* IN ISSUE 110.

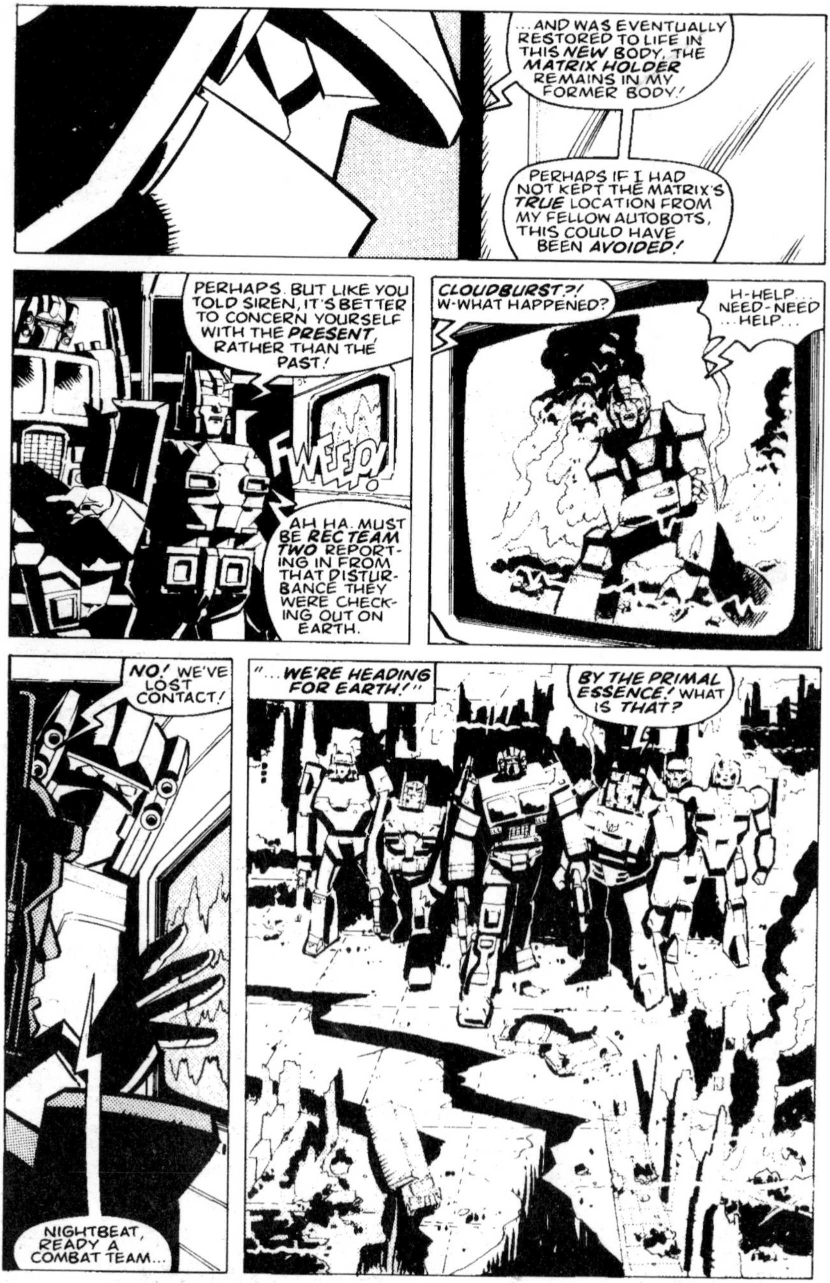
...AND WAS EVENTUALLY RESTORED TO LIFE IN THIS NEW BODY, THE MATRIX HOLDER REMAINS IN MY FORMER BODY!
PERHAPS IF I HAD NOT KEPT THE MATRIX'S TRUE LOCATION FROM MY FELLOW AUTOBOTS, THIS COULD HAVE BEEN AVOIDED!
PERHAPS. BUT LIKE YOU TOLD SIREN, IT'S BETTER TO CONCERN YOURSELF WITH THE PRESENT, RATHER THAN THE PAST!
FWEEP!
AH HA. MUST BE REC TEAM TWO REPORTING IN FROM THAT DISTURBANCE THEY WERE CHECKING OUT ON EARTH.
CLOUDBURST?! W-WHAT HAPPENED?
H-HELP... NEED-NEED ...HELP...
NO! WE'VE LOST CONTACT!
NIGHTBEAT, READY A COMBAT TEAM...
"...WE'RE HEADING FOR EARTH!"
BY THE PRIMAL ESSENCE! WHAT IS THAT?

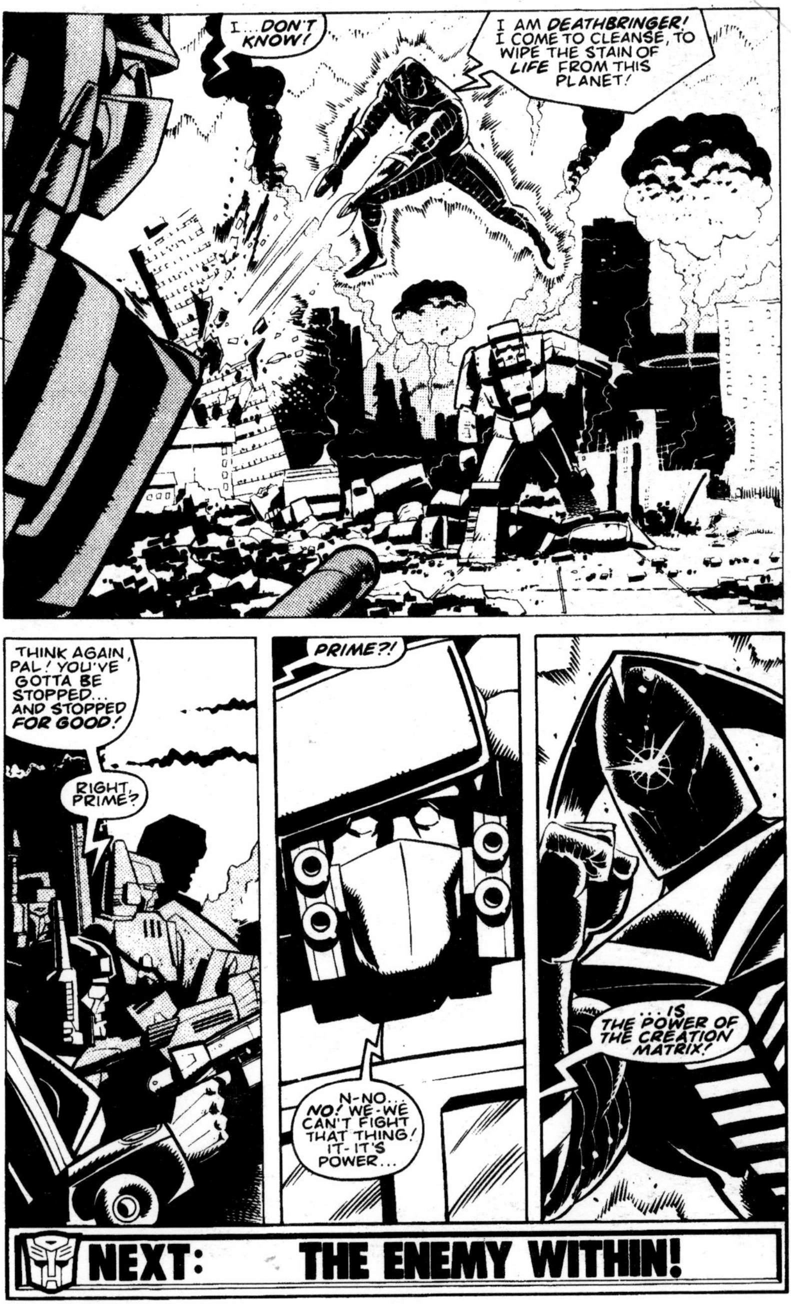
I... DON'T KNOW!
I AM DEATHBRINGER! I COME TO CLEANSE, TO WIPE THE STAIN OF LIFE FROM THIS PLANET!
THINK AGAIN, PAL! YOU'VE GOTTA BE STOPPED... AND STOPPED FOR GOOD!
RIGHT, PRIME?
PRIME?!
N-NO... NO! WE-WE CAN'T FIGHT THAT THING! IT-IT'S POWER...
...IS THE POWER OF THE CREATION MATRIX!
NEXT: THE ENEMY WITHIN!

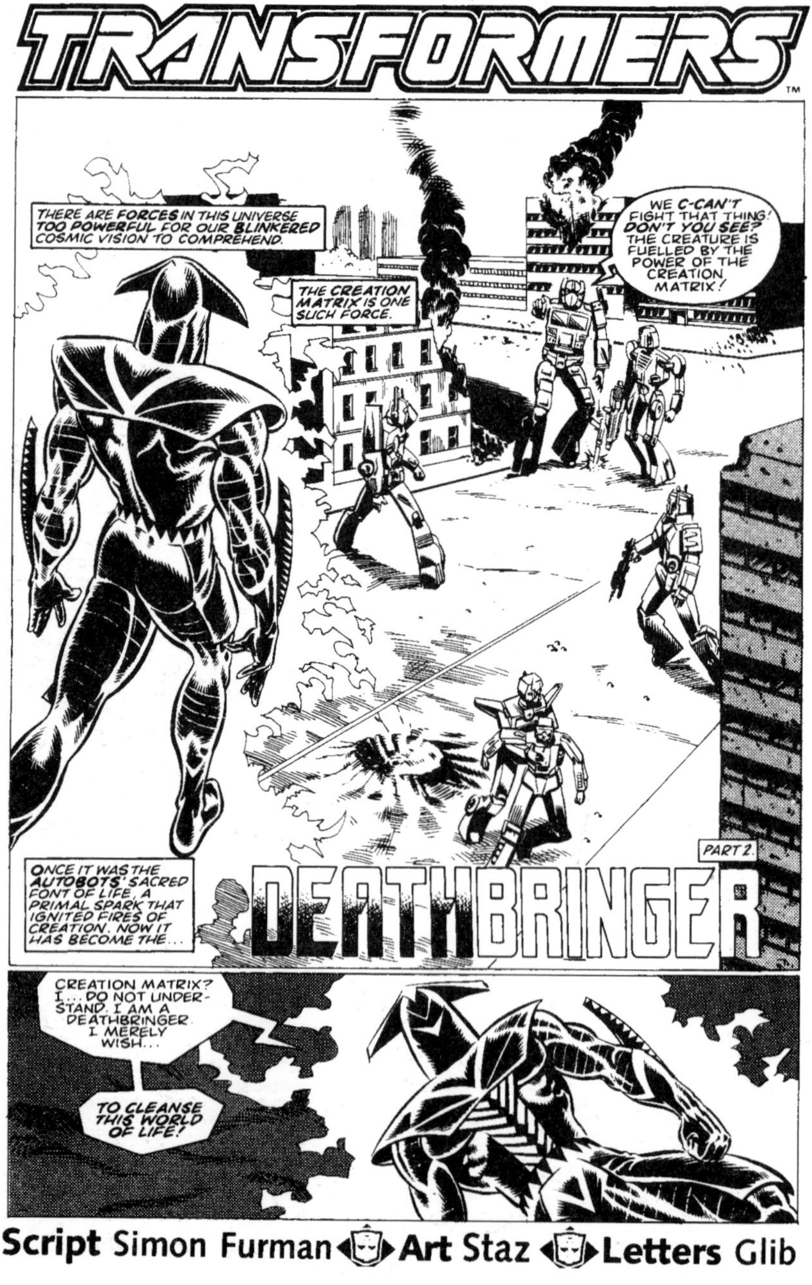
TRANSFORMERS
THERE ARE FORCES IN THIS UNIVERSE TOO POWERFUL FOR OUR BLINKERED COSMIC VISION TO COMPREHEND.
THE CREATION MATRIX IS ONE SUCH FORCE.
WE C-CAN'T FIGHT THAT THING! DON'T YOU SEE? THE CREATURE IS FUELLED BY THE POWER OF THE CREATION MATRIX!
PART 2.
ONCE IT WAS THE AUTOBOTS' SACRED FONT OF LIFE, A PRIMAL SPARK THAT IGNITED FIRES OF CREATION. NOW IT HAS BECOME THE...
DEATHBRINGER
CREATION MATRIX? I... DO NOT UNDERSTAND. I AM A DEATHBRINGER. I MERELY WISH...
TO CLEANSE THIS WORLD OF LIFE!

Script Simon Furman **Art** Staz **Letters** Glib

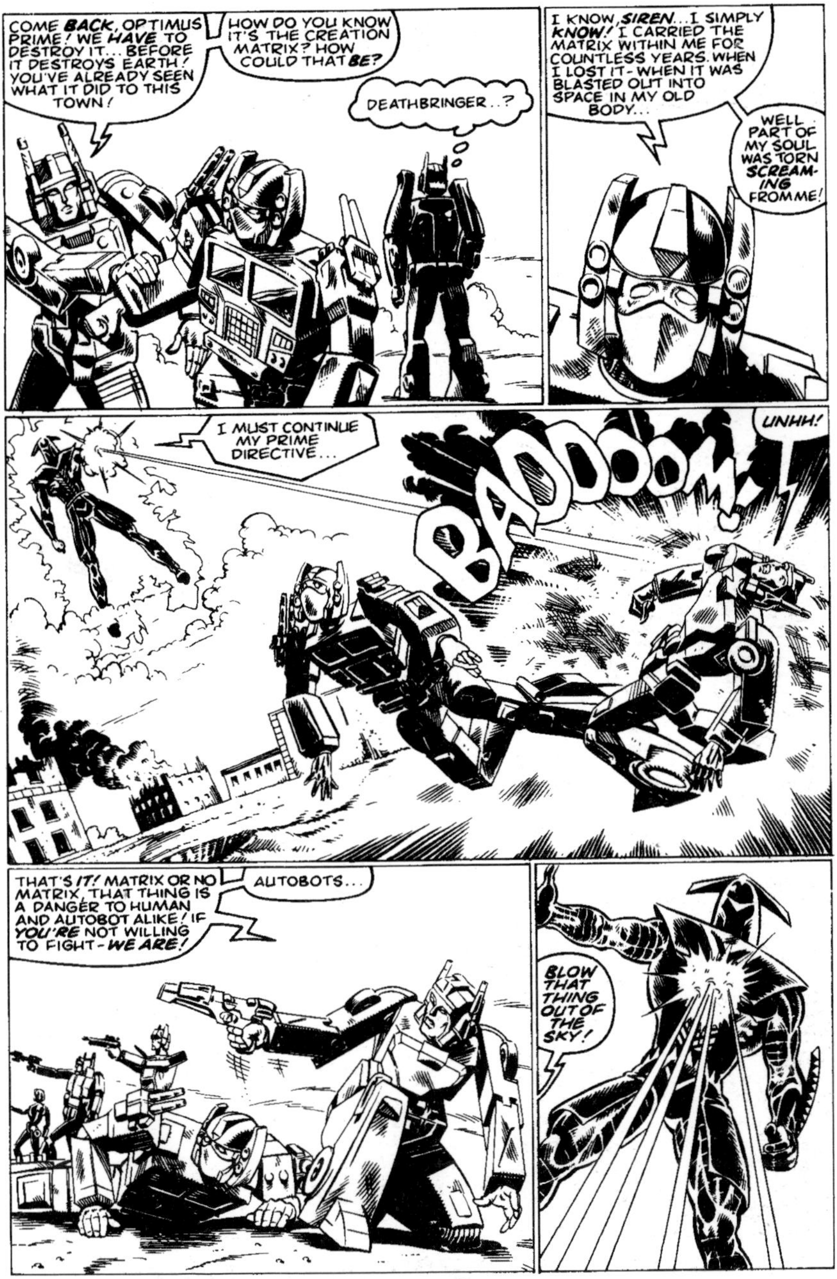
COME BACK, OPTIMUS PRIME! WE HAVE TO DESTROY IT... BEFORE IT DESTROYS EARTH! YOU'VE ALREADY SEEN WHAT IT DID TO THIS TOWN!
HOW DO YOU KNOW IT'S THE CREATION MATRIX? HOW COULD THAT BE?
DEATHBRINGER..?
I KNOW, SIREN... I SIMPLY KNOW! I CARRIED THE MATRIX WITHIN ME FOR COUNTLESS YEARS. WHEN I LOST IT- WHEN IT WAS BLASTED OUT INTO SPACE IN MY OLD BODY...
WELL PART OF MY SOUL WAS TORN SCREAMING FROM ME!
I MUST CONTINUE MY PRIME DIRECTIVE...
BADOOOM!
UNHH!
THAT'S IT! MATRIX OR NO MATRIX, THAT THING IS A DANGER TO HUMAN AND AUTOBOT ALIKE! IF YOU'RE NOT WILLING TO FIGHT- WE ARE!
AUTOBOTS...
BLOW THAT THING OUT OF THE SKY!

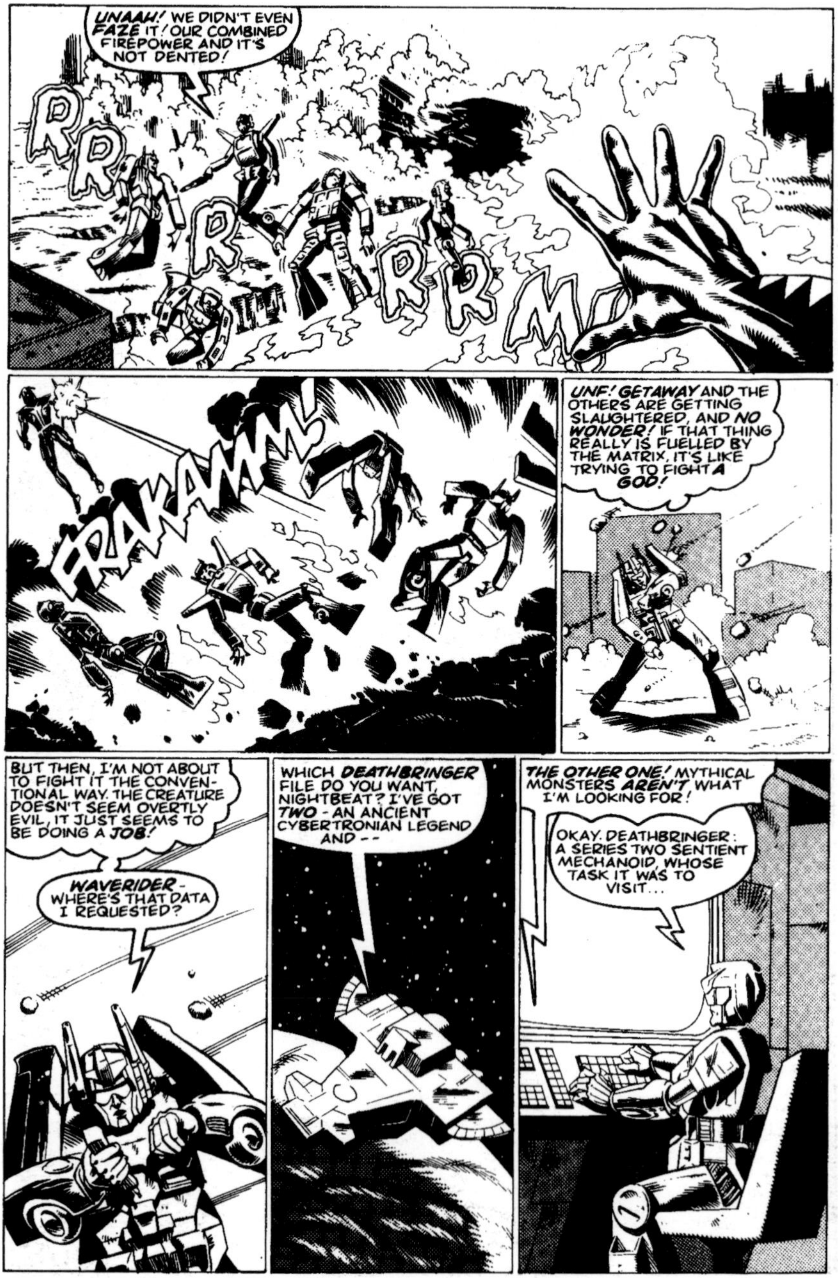
UNAAH! WE DIDN'T EVEN FAZE IT! OUR COMBINED FIREPOWER AND IT'S NOT DENTED!
RRRRRRMM
KRAKAMM!
UNF! GETAWAY AND THE OTHERS ARE GETTING SLAUGHTERED, AND NO WONDER! IF THAT THING REALLY IS FUELLED BY THE MATRIX, IT'S LIKE TRYING TO FIGHT A GOD!
BUT THEN, I'M NOT ABOUT TO FIGHT IT THE CONVENTIONAL WAY. THE CREATURE DOESN'T SEEM OVERTLY EVIL, IT JUST SEEMS TO BE DOING A JOB!
WAVERIDER - WHERE'S THAT DATA I REQUESTED?
WHICH DEATHBRINGER FILE DO YOU WANT, NIGHTBEAT? I'VE GOT TWO - AN ANCIENT CYBERTRONIAN LEGEND AND --
THE OTHER ONE! MYTHICAL MONSTERS AREN'T WHAT I'M LOOKING FOR!
OKAY. DEATHBRINGER: A SERIES TWO SENTIENT MECHANOID, WHOSE TASK IT WAS TO VISIT...

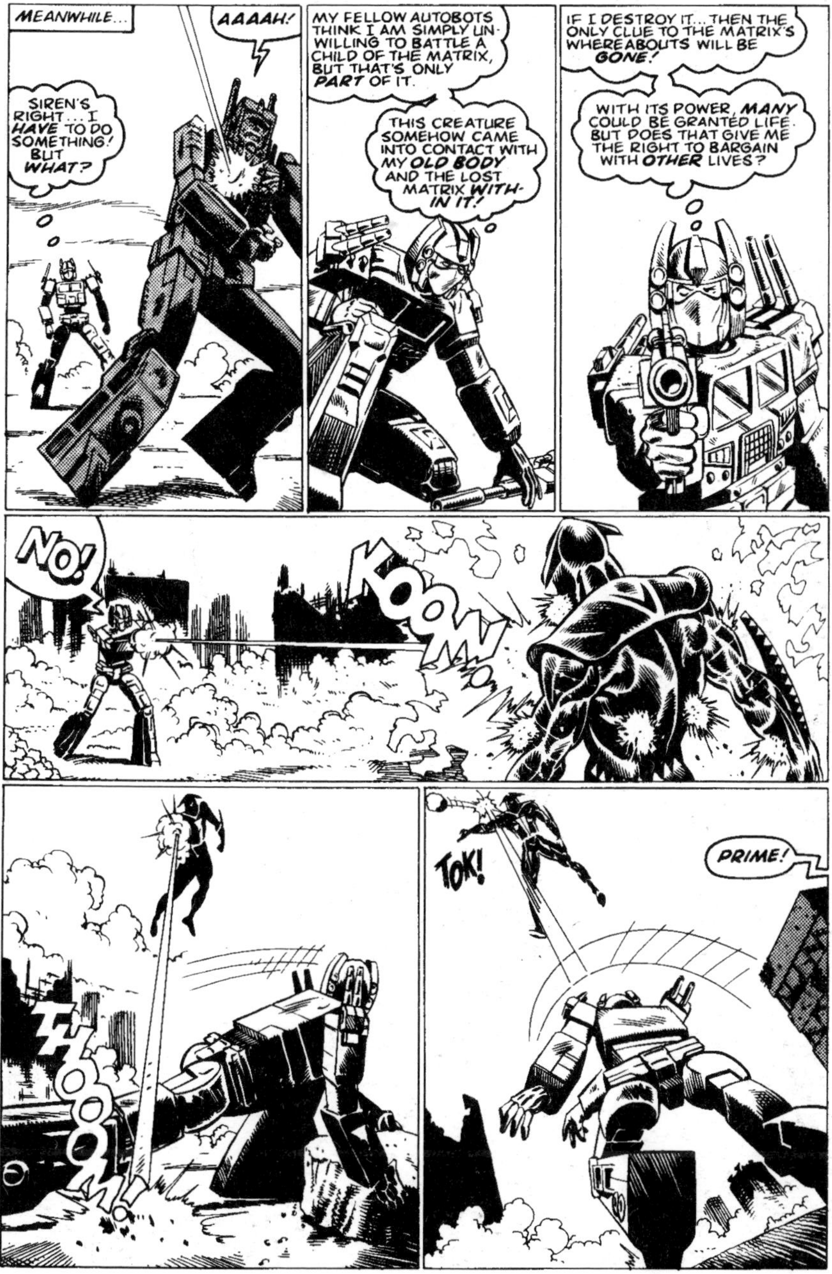
MEANWHILE...
AAAAH!
SIREN'S RIGHT... I HAVE TO DO SOMETHING! BUT WHAT?
MY FELLOW AUTOBOTS THINK I AM SIMPLY UNWILLING TO BATTLE A CHILD OF THE MATRIX, BUT THAT'S ONLY PART OF IT.
THIS CREATURE SOMEHOW CAME INTO CONTACT WITH MY OLD BODY AND THE LOST MATRIX WITHIN IT!
IF I DESTROY IT... THEN THE ONLY CLUE TO THE MATRIX'S WHEREABOUTS WILL BE GONE!
WITH ITS POWER, MANY COULD BE GRANTED LIFE. BUT DOES THAT GIVE ME THE RIGHT TO BARGAIN WITH OTHER LIVES?
NO!
KOOOOM
THOOOOM!
TOK!
PRIME!

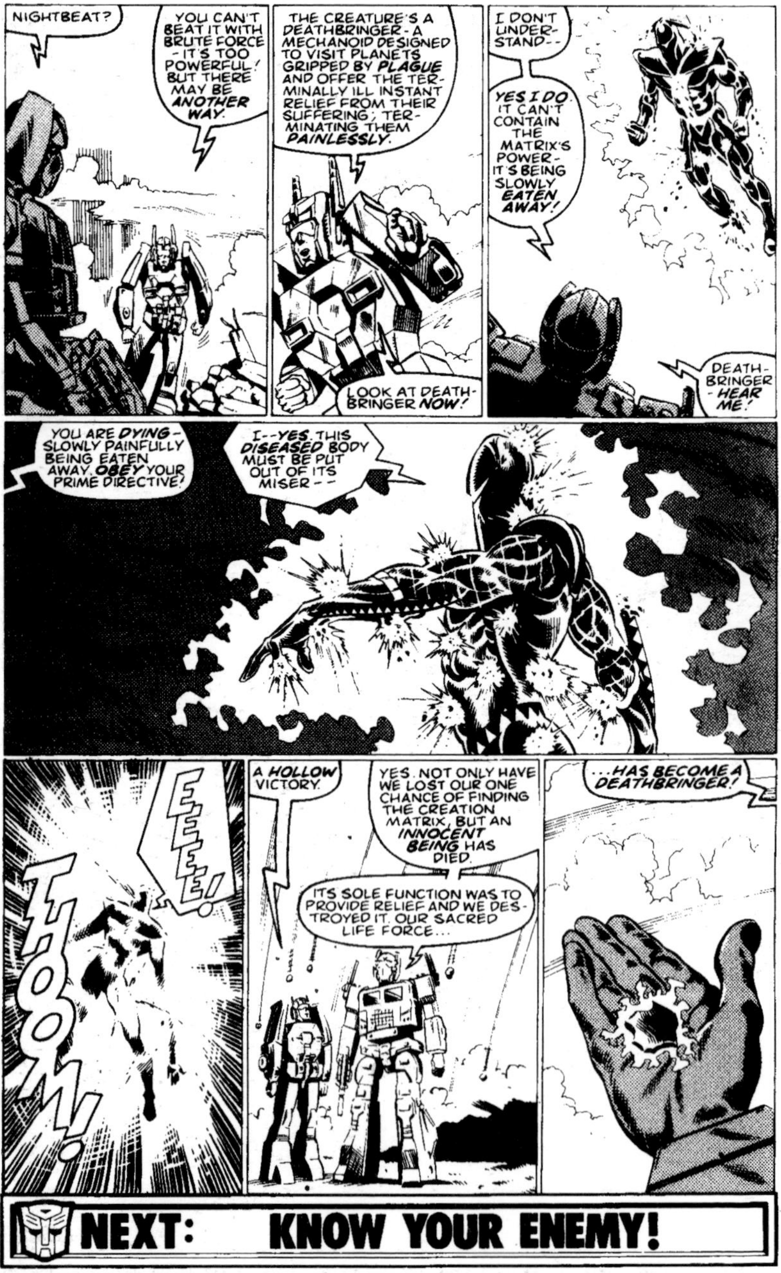
NIGHTBEAT?
YOU CAN'T BEAT IT WITH BRUTE FORCE - IT'S TOO POWERFUL! BUT THERE MAY BE ANOTHER WAY.
THE CREATURE'S A DEATHBRINGER - A MECHANOID DESIGNED TO VISIT PLANETS GRIPPED BY PLAGUE AND OFFER THE TERMINALLY ILL INSTANT RELIEF FROM THEIR SUFFERING; TERMINATING THEM PAINLESSLY.
LOOK AT DEATHBRINGER NOW!
I DON'T UNDERSTAND--
YES I DO. IT CAN'T CONTAIN THE MATRIX'S POWER - IT'S BEING SLOWLY EATEN AWAY!
DEATHBRINGER - HEAR ME!
YOU ARE DYING - SLOWLY PAINFULLY BEING EATEN AWAY. OBEY YOUR PRIME DIRECTIVE!
I--YES. THIS DISEASED BODY MUST BE PUT OUT OF ITS MISER--
EEEEE!
THOOOM!
A HOLLOW VICTORY.
YES. NOT ONLY HAVE WE LOST OUR ONE CHANCE OF FINDING THE CREATION MATRIX, BUT AN INNOCENT BEING HAS DIED.
ITS SOLE FUNCTION WAS TO PROVIDE RELIEF AND WE DESTROYED IT. OUR SACRED LIFE FORCE...
...HAS BECOME A DEATHBRINGER!

NEXT: KNOW YOUR ENEMY!

TRANSFORMERS™

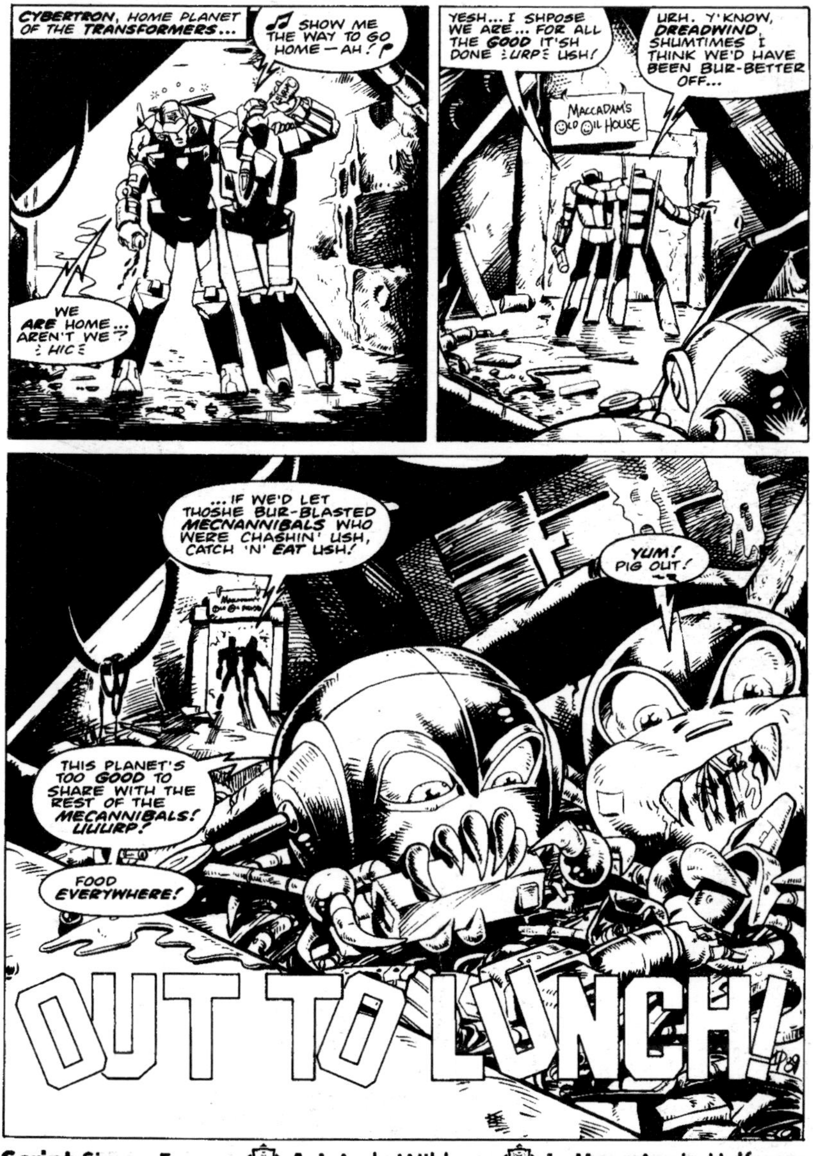
CYBERTRON, HOME PLANET OF THE TRANSFORMERS...
♫ SHOW ME THE WAY TO GO HOME—AH! ♪
WE ARE HOME... AREN'T WE? :HIC:
YESH... I SHPOSE WE ARE... FOR ALL THE GOOD IT'SH DONE :URP: USH!
URH. Y'KNOW, DREADWIND, SHUMTIMES I THINK WE'D HAVE BEEN BUR-BETTER OFF...
MACCADAM'S OLD OIL HOUSE
...IF WE'D LET THOSHE BUR-BLASTED MECNANNIBALS WHO WERE CHASHIN' USH, CATCH 'N' EAT USH!
YUM! PIG OUT!
THIS PLANET'S TOO GOOD TO SHARE WITH THE REST OF THE MECANNIBALS! UUURP!
FOOD EVERYWHERE!
OUT TO LUNCH!

Script Simon Furman **Art** Andy Wildman **Letters** Annie Halfacree

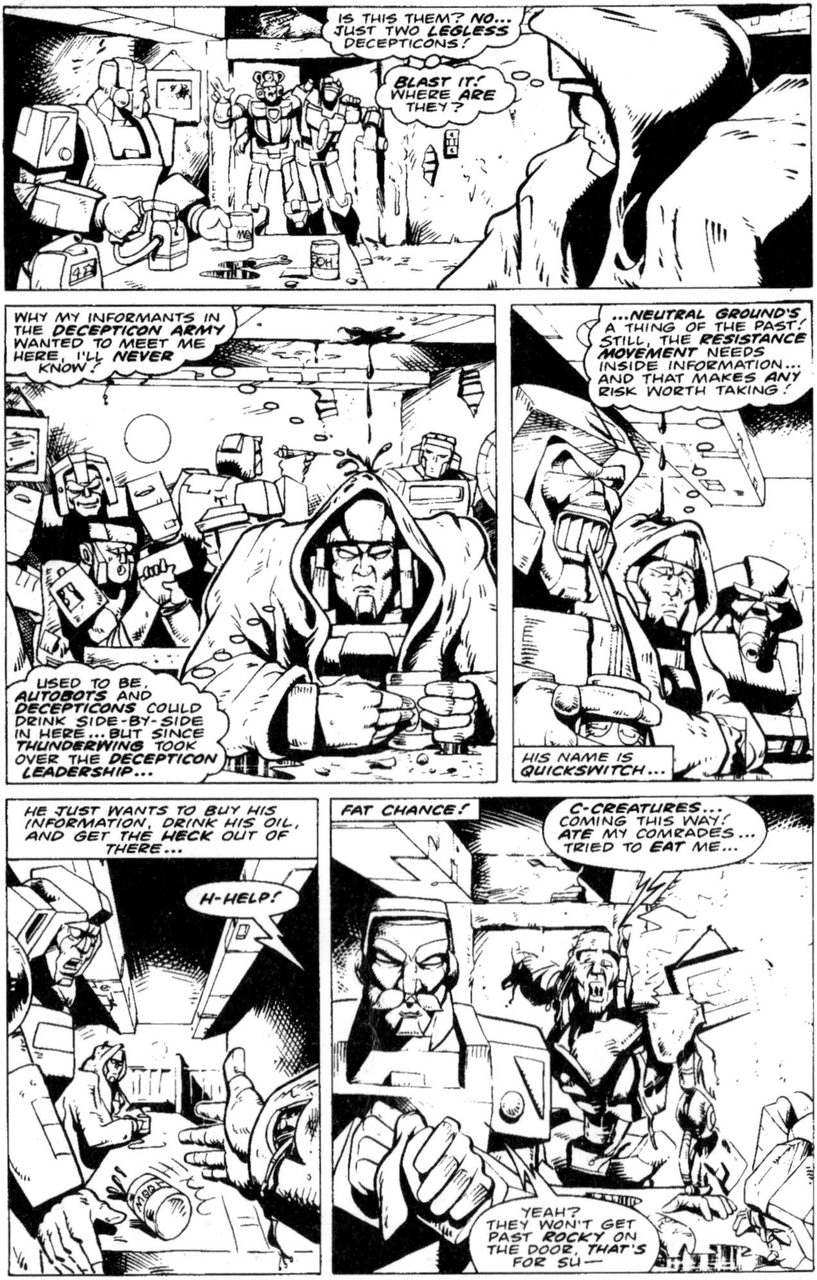
IS THIS THEM? NO... JUST TWO LEGLESS DECEPTICONS!
BLAST IT! WHERE ARE THEY?
WHY MY INFORMANTS IN THE DECEPTICON ARMY WANTED TO MEET ME HERE, I'LL NEVER KNOW!
USED TO BE, AUTOBOTS AND DECEPTICONS COULD DRINK SIDE-BY-SIDE IN HERE... BUT SINCE THUNDERWING TOOK OVER THE DECEPTICON LEADERSHIP...
...NEUTRAL GROUND'S A THING OF THE PAST! STILL, THE RESISTANCE MOVEMENT NEEDS INSIDE INFORMATION... AND THAT MAKES ANY RISK WORTH TAKING!
HIS NAME IS QUICKSWITCH...
HE JUST WANTS TO BUY HIS INFORMATION, DRINK HIS OIL, AND GET THE HECK OUT OF THERE...
H-HELP!
FAT CHANCE!
C-CREATURES... COMING THIS WAY! ATE MY COMRADES... TRIED TO EAT ME...
YEAH? THEY WON'T GET PAST ROCKY ON THE DOOR, THAT'S FOR SU—

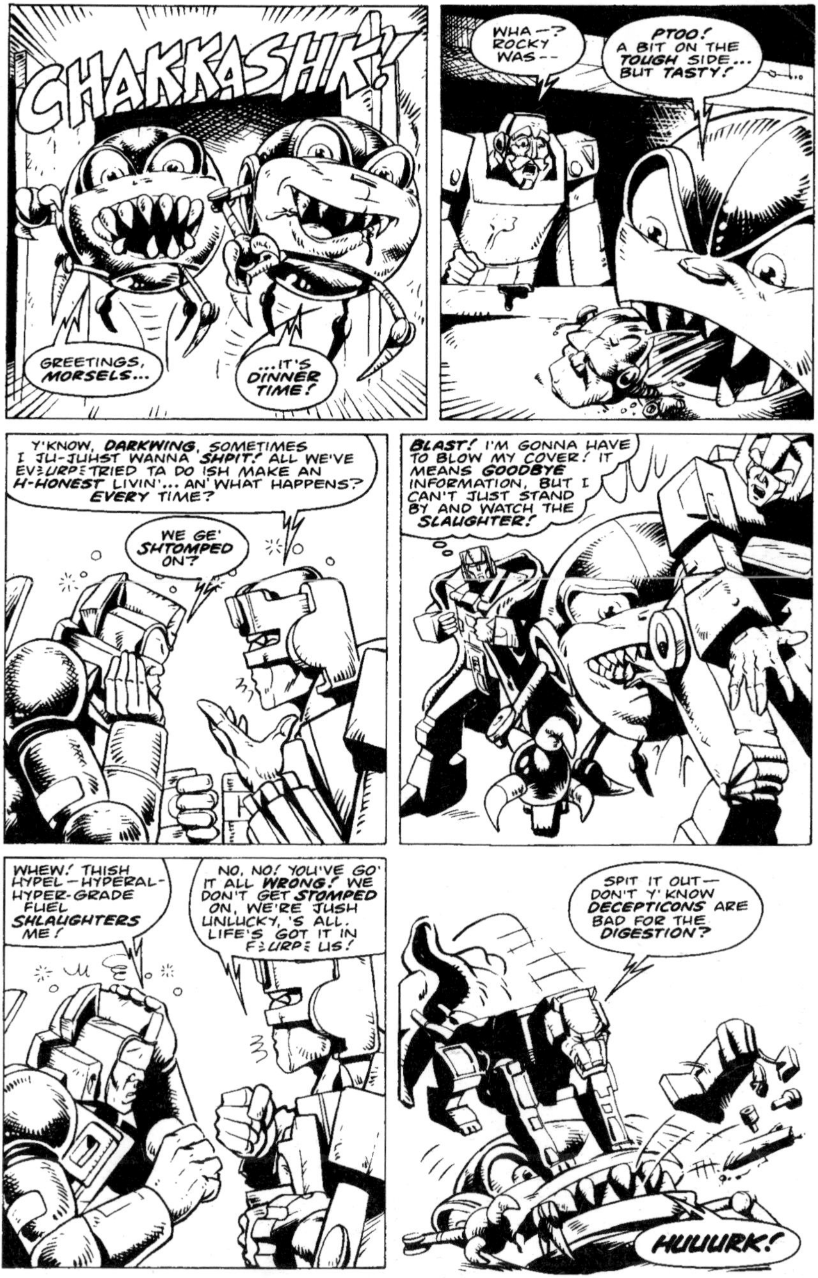
CHAKKASHK!
GREETINGS, MORSELS...
...IT'S DINNER TIME!
WHA--? ROCKY WAS--
PTOO! A BIT ON THE TOUGH SIDE... BUT TASTY!
Y'KNOW, DARKWING, SOMETIMES I JU-JUHST WANNA SHPIT! ALL WE'VE EV-URP-TRIED TA DO ISH MAKE AN H-HONEST LIVIN'... AN' WHAT HAPPENS? EVERY TIME?
WE GE' SHTOMPED ON?
BLAST! I'M GONNA HAVE TO BLOW MY COVER! IT MEANS GOODBYE INFORMATION, BUT I CAN'T JUST STAND BY AND WATCH THE SLAUGHTER!
WHEW! THISH HYPEL-HYPERAL-HYPER-GRADE FUEL SHLAUGHTERS ME!
NO, NO! YOU'VE GO' IT ALL WRONG! WE DON'T GET STOMPED ON, WE'RE JUSH UNLUCKY, 'S ALL. LIFE'S GOT IT IN F-URP-US!
SPIT IT OUT-- DON'T Y'KNOW DECEPTICONS ARE BAD FOR THE DIGESTION?
HUUURK!

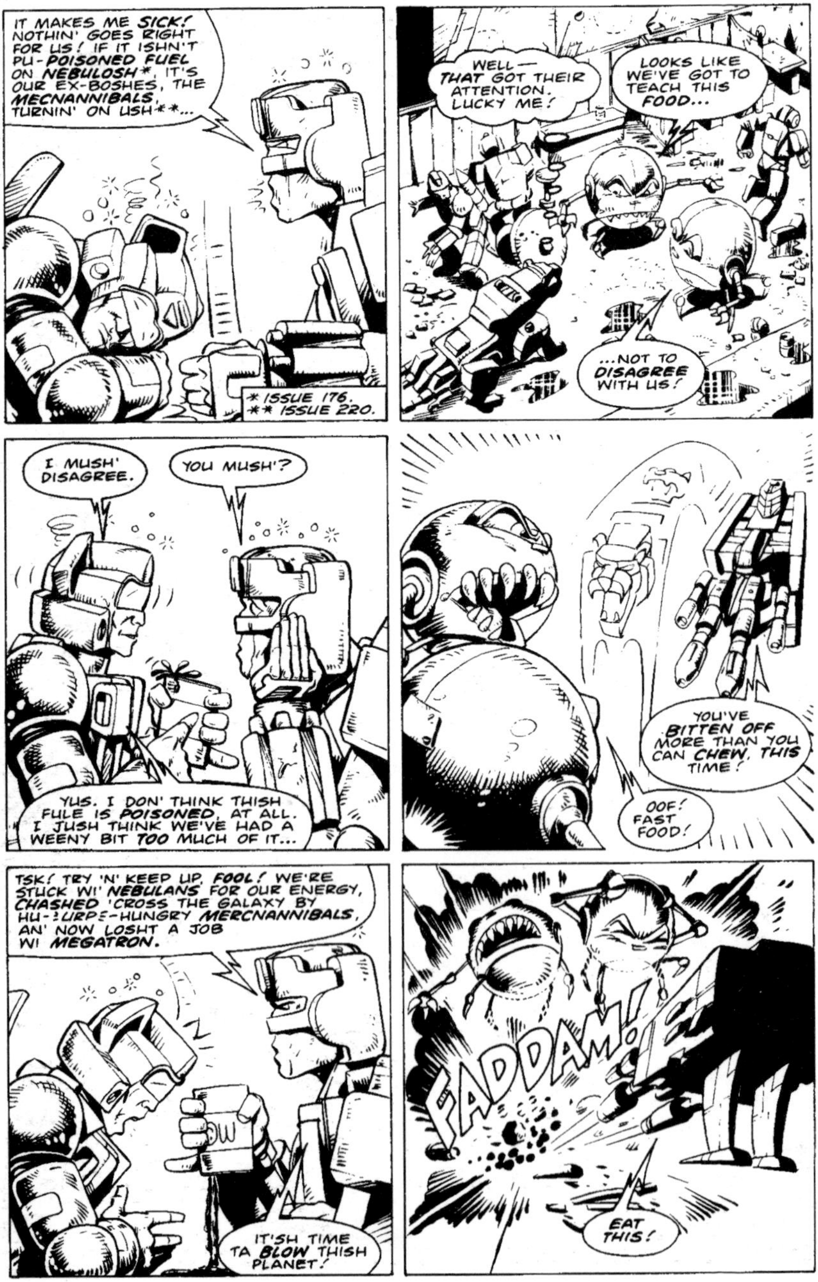

IT MAKES ME SICK! NOTHIN' GOES RIGHT FOR US! IF IT ISHN'T PU-POISONED FUEL ON NEBULOSH*, IT'S OUR EX-BOSHES, THE MECNANNIBALS, TURNIN' ON USH**...
* ISSUE 176.
** ISSUE 220.
WELL— THAT GOT THEIR ATTENTION. LUCKY ME!
LOOKS LIKE WE'VE GOT TO TEACH THIS FOOD...
...NOT TO DISAGREE WITH US!
I MUSH' DISAGREE.
YOU MUSH'?
YUS. I DON' THINK THISH FULE IS POISONED, AT ALL. I JUSH THINK WE'VE HAD A WEENY BIT TOO MUCH OF IT...
YOU'VE BITTEN OFF MORE THAN YOU CAN CHEW, THIS TIME!
OOF! FAST FOOD!
TSK! TRY 'N' KEEP UP, FOOL! WE'RE STUCK WI' NEBULANS FOR OUR ENERGY, CHASHED 'CROSS THE GALAXY BY HU-BURPE-HUNGRY MERCNANNIBALS, AN' NOW LOSHT A JOB WI MEGATRON.
IT'SH TIME TA BLOW THISH PLANET!
FADDAM!
EAT THIS!

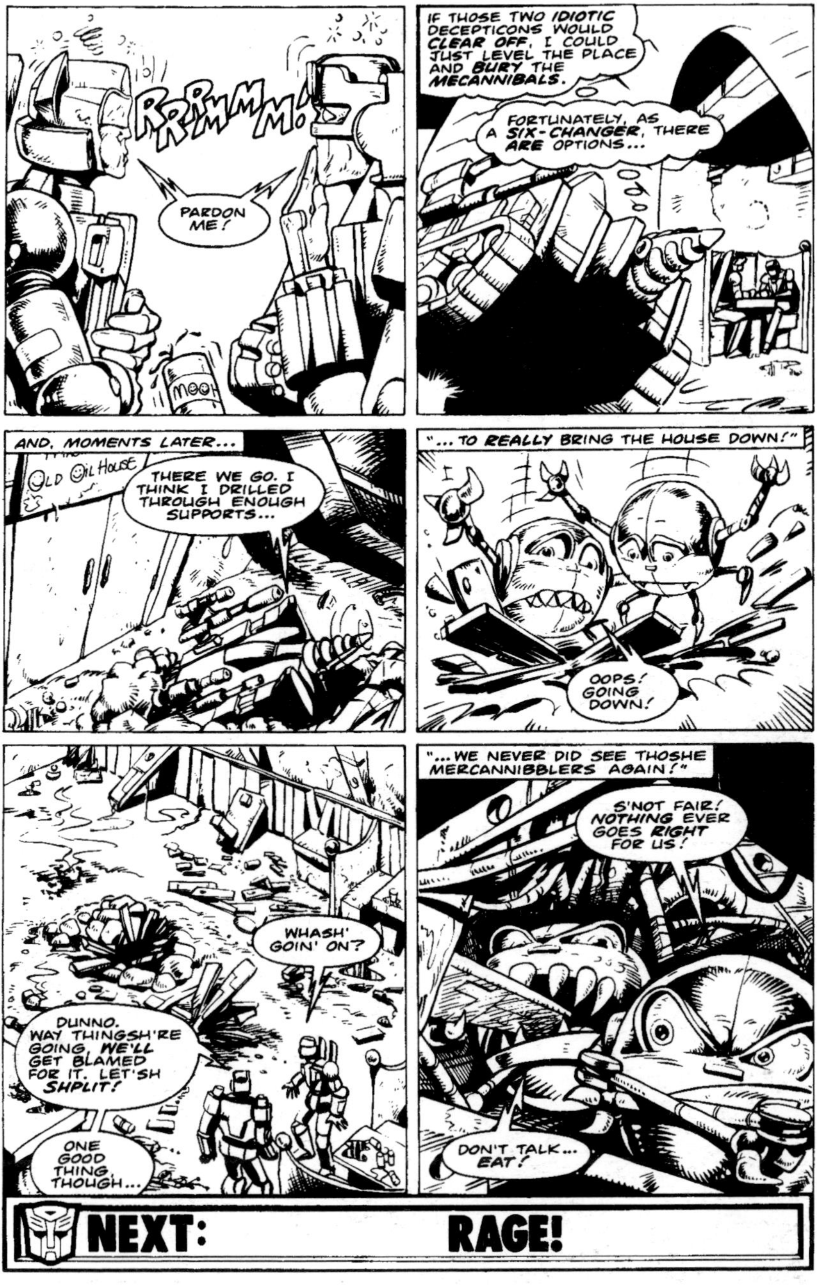
RRRMMMM!
PARDON ME!
MOO
IF THOSE TWO IDIOTIC DECEPTICONS WOULD CLEAR OFF, I COULD JUST LEVEL THE PLACE AND BURY THE MECANNIBALS.
FORTUNATELY, AS A SIX-CHANGER, THERE ARE OPTIONS...
AND, MOMENTS LATER...
OLD OIL HOUSE
THERE WE GO. I THINK I DRILLED THROUGH ENOUGH SUPPORTS...
"... TO REALLY BRING THE HOUSE DOWN!"
OOPS! GOING DOWN!
WHASH' GOIN' ON?
DUNNO. WAY THINGSH'RE GOING WE'LL GET BLAMED FOR IT. LET'SH SHPLIT!
ONE GOOD THING, THOUGH...
"... WE NEVER DID SEE THOSHE MERCANNIBBLERS AGAIN!"
S'NOT FAIR! NOTHING EVER GOES RIGHT FOR US!
DON'T TALK... EAT!
NEXT: RAGE!

TRANSFORMERS ™

BELOW THE SURFACE OF THE TRANSFORMERS' HOMEWORLD...

BELOW CYBERTRON'S LONG DISUSED SEWER SYSTEM...

THERE IS...

UNDERWORLD!

A WORLD OF TOWERING, TWISTED METAL **SCREAMING** AT SHADOWS THAT **WRITHE** IN **UNHOLY** SILENCE EMBRACING THE **UNWARY** IN **CIRCUIT-CHILLING** TENDRILS OF MIST.

A WHOLE WORLD OF **PAIN** AND **HURT.**

COME OUT, COME OUT, **WHEREVER** YOU ARE. LET'S **PARTYYY!**

Script Simon Furman ◆ **Art** Jeff Anderson ◆ **Letters** Helen Stone

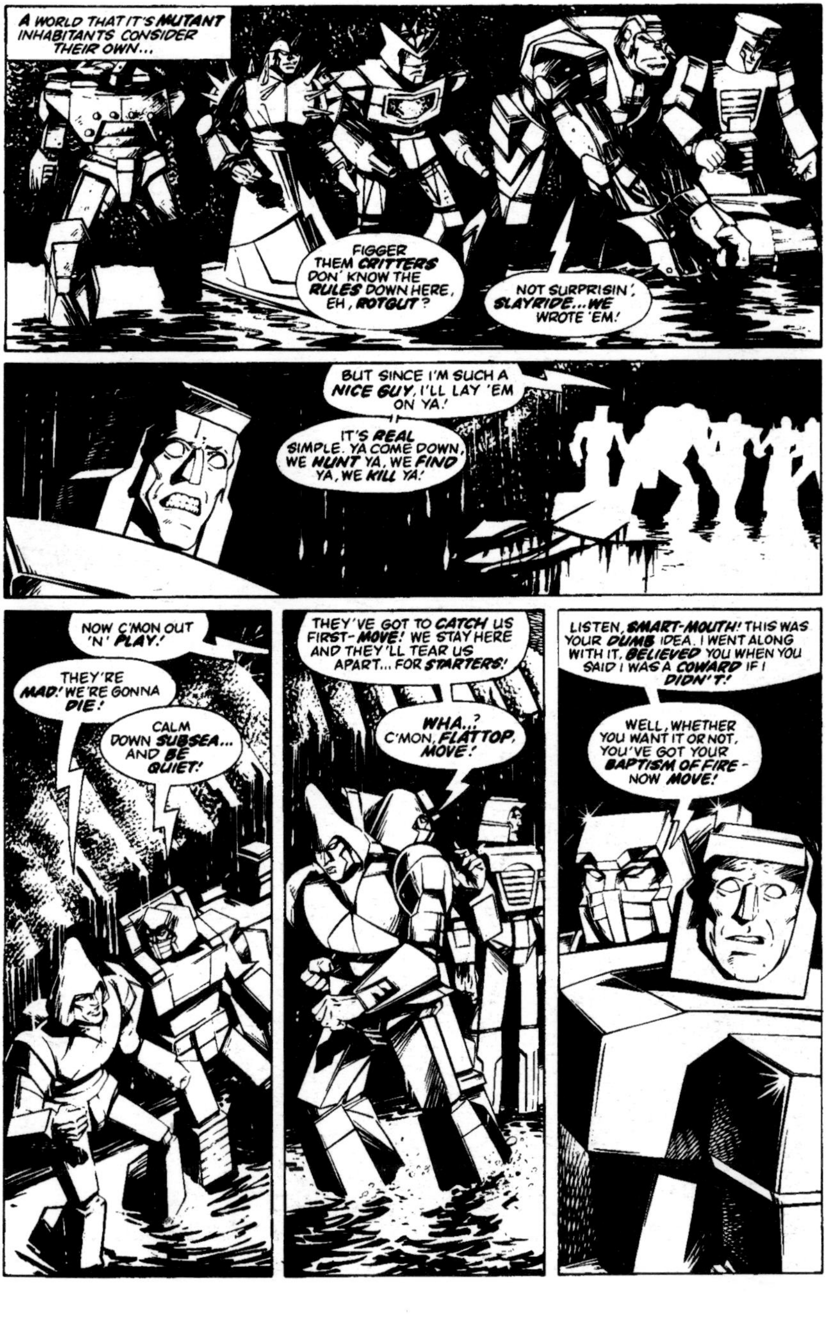
A WORLD THAT IT'S MUTANT INHABITANTS CONSIDER THEIR OWN...
FIGGER THEM CRITTERS DON' KNOW THE RULES DOWN HERE, EH, ROTGUT?
NOT SURPRISIN', SLAYRIDE... WE WROTE 'EM!
BUT SINCE I'M SUCH A NICE GUY, I'LL LAY 'EM ON YA!
IT'S REAL SIMPLE. YA COME DOWN, WE HUNT YA, WE FIND YA, WE KILL YA!
NOW C'MON OUT 'N' PLAY!
THEY'RE MAD! WE'RE GONNA DIE!
CALM DOWN SUBSEA... AND BE QUIET!
THEY'VE GOT TO CATCH US FIRST- MOVE! WE STAY HERE AND THEY'LL TEAR US APART... FOR STARTERS!
WHA..? C'MON, FLATTOP, MOVE!
LISTEN, SMART-MOUTH! THIS WAS YOUR DUMB IDEA. I WENT ALONG WITH IT. BELIEVED YOU WHEN YOU SAID I WAS A COWARD IF I DIDN'T!
WELL, WHETHER YOU WANT IT OR NOT, YOU'VE GOT YOUR BAPTISM OF FIRE - NOW MOVE!

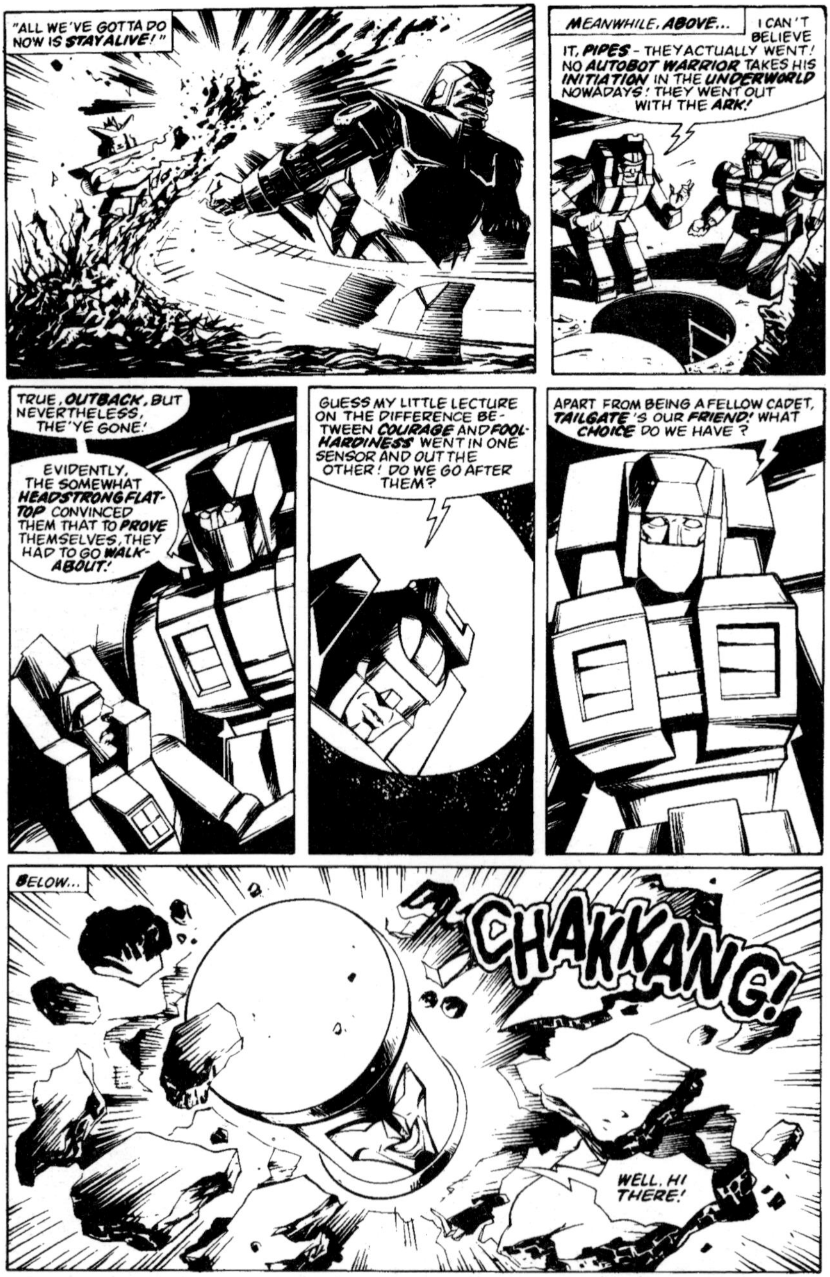
"ALL WE'VE GOTTA DO NOW IS STAY ALIVE!"
MEANWHILE, ABOVE...
I CAN'T BELIEVE IT, PIPES - THEY ACTUALLY WENT! NO AUTOBOT WARRIOR TAKES HIS INITIATION IN THE UNDERWORLD NOWADAYS! THEY WENT OUT WITH THE ARK!
TRUE, OUTBACK, BUT NEVERTHELESS, THEY'VE GONE!
EVIDENTLY, THE SOMEWHAT HEADSTRONG FLAT-TOP CONVINCED THEM THAT TO PROVE THEMSELVES, THEY HAD TO GO WALK-ABOUT!
GUESS MY LITTLE LECTURE ON THE DIFFERENCE BE-TWEEN COURAGE AND FOOL-HARDINESS WENT IN ONE SENSOR AND OUT THE OTHER! DO WE GO AFTER THEM?
APART FROM BEING A FELLOW CADET, TAILGATE'S OUR FRIEND! WHAT CHOICE DO WE HAVE?
BELOW...
CHAKKANG!
WELL, HI THERE!

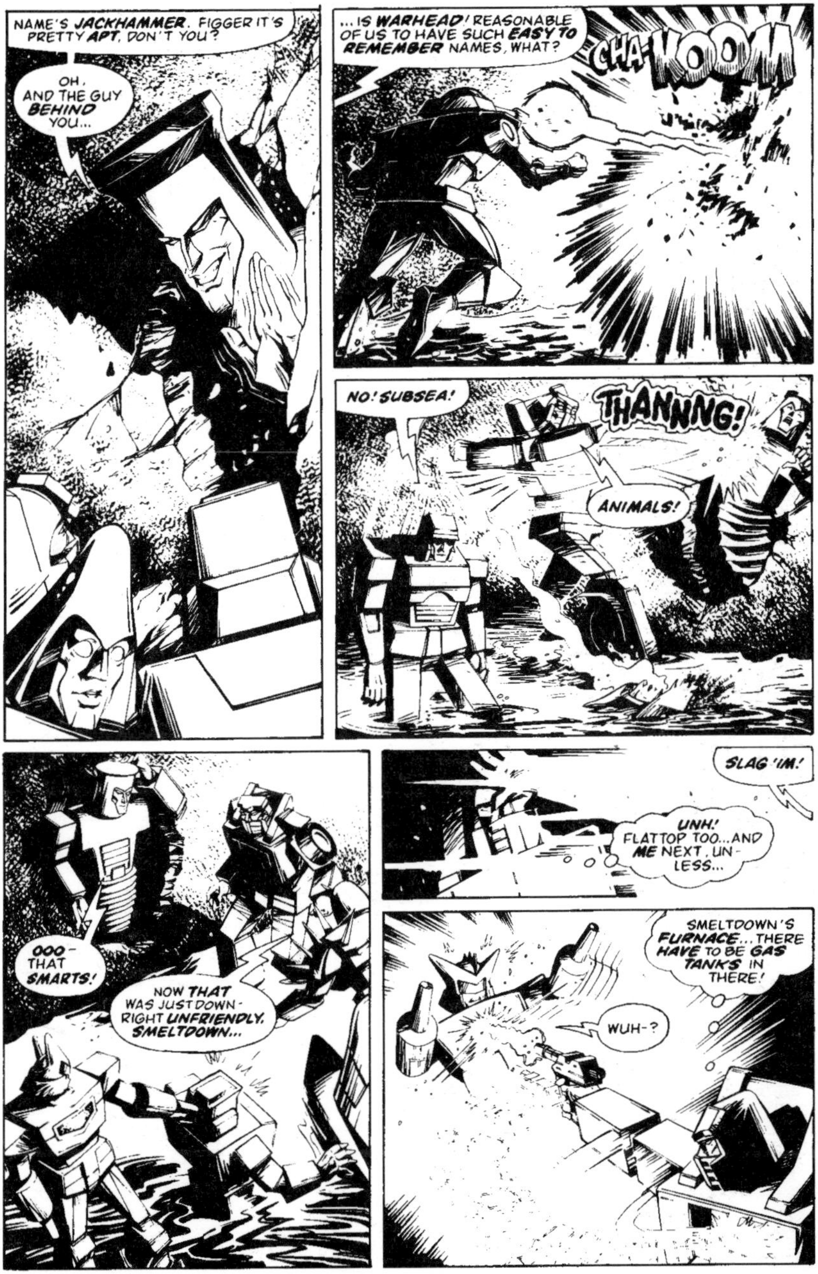
NAME'S JACKHAMMER. FIGGER IT'S PRETTY APT, DON'T YOU?
OH, AND THE GUY BEHIND YOU...
...IS WARHEAD! REASONABLE OF US TO HAVE SUCH EASY TO REMEMBER NAMES, WHAT?
CHA-KOOOM
NO! SUBSEA!
THANNNG!
ANIMALS!
OOO-THAT SMARTS!
NOW THAT WAS JUST DOWN-RIGHT UNFRIENDLY, SMELTDOWN...
SLAG 'IM!
UNH! FLATTOP TOO...AND ME NEXT, UN-LESS...
SMELTDOWN'S FURNACE...THERE HAVE TO BE GAS TANKS IN THERE!
WUH-?

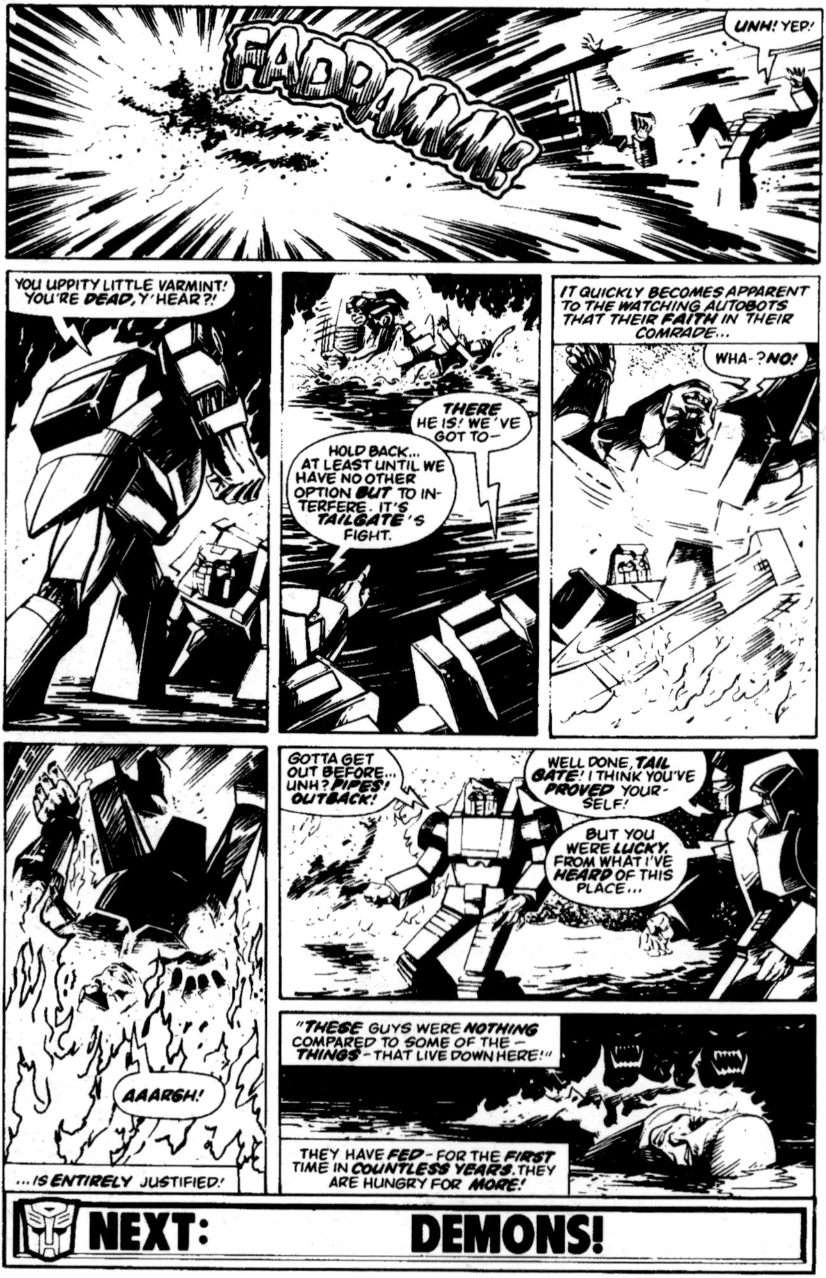
FADDAMM!
UNH! YEP!
YOU UPPITY LITTLE VARMINT! YOU'RE DEAD, Y'HEAR?!
THERE HE IS! WE'VE GOT TO-
HOLD BACK... AT LEAST UNTIL WE HAVE NO OTHER OPTION BUT TO INTERFERE. IT'S TAILGATE'S FIGHT.
IT QUICKLY BECOMES APPARENT TO THE WATCHING AUTOBOTS THAT THEIR FAITH IN THEIR COMRADE...
WHA-? NO!
AAARGH!
...IS ENTIRELY JUSTIFIED!
GOTTA GET OUT BEFORE... UNH? PIPES! OUTBACK!
WELL DONE, TAILGATE! I THINK YOU'VE PROVED YOURSELF!
BUT YOU WERE LUCKY. FROM WHAT I'VE HEARD OF THIS PLACE...
"THESE GUYS WERE NOTHING COMPARED TO SOME OF THE — THINGS — THAT LIVE DOWN HERE!"
THEY HAVE FED — FOR THE FIRST TIME IN COUNTLESS YEARS. THEY ARE HUNGRY FOR MORE!

NEXT: DEMONS!

TRANSFORMERS™

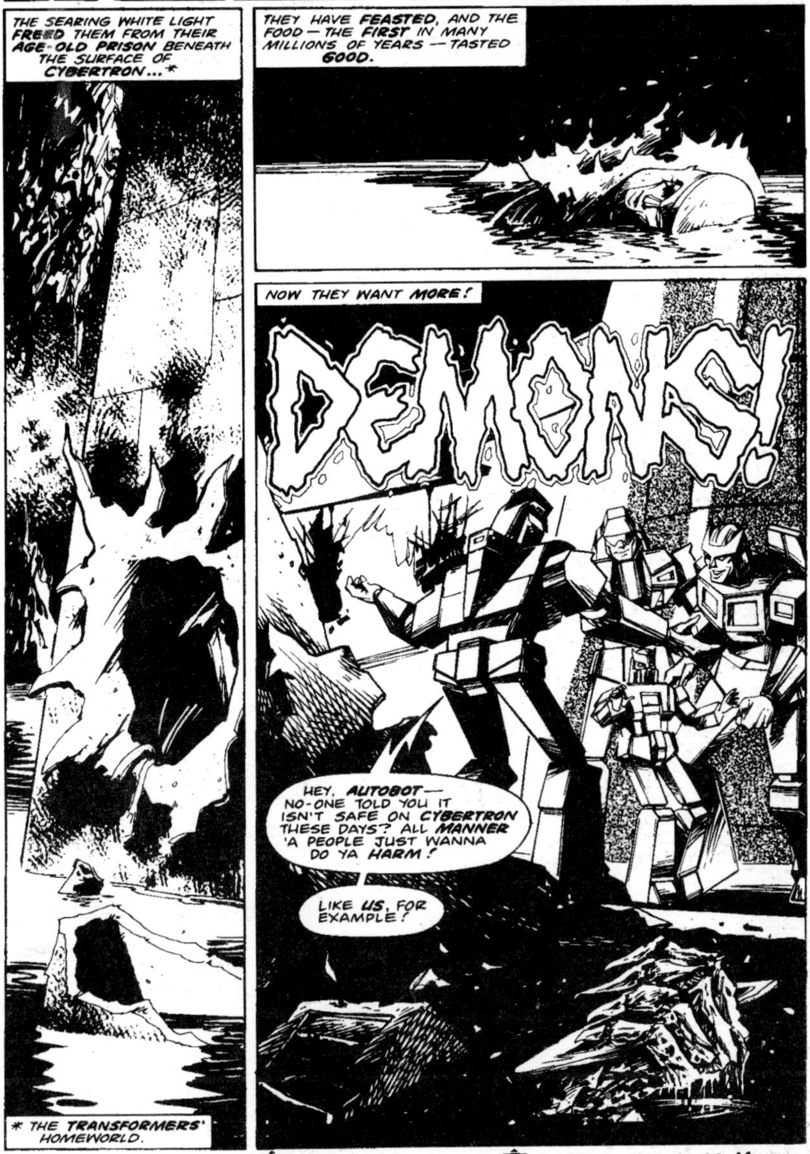

THE SEARING WHITE LIGHT FREED THEM FROM THEIR AGE-OLD PRISON BENEATH THE SURFACE OF CYBERTRON...*
THEY HAVE FEASTED, AND THE FOOD — THE FIRST IN MANY MILLIONS OF YEARS — TASTED GOOD.
NOW THEY WANT MORE!
DEMONS!
HEY, AUTOBOT— NO-ONE TOLD YOU IT ISN'T SAFE ON CYBERTRON THESE DAYS? ALL MANNER 'A PEOPLE JUST WANNA DO YA HARM!
LIKE US, FOR EXAMPLE!
* THE TRANSFORMERS' HOMEWORLD.

Script Simon Furman **Art** Jeff Anderson **Letters** Annie Halfacree

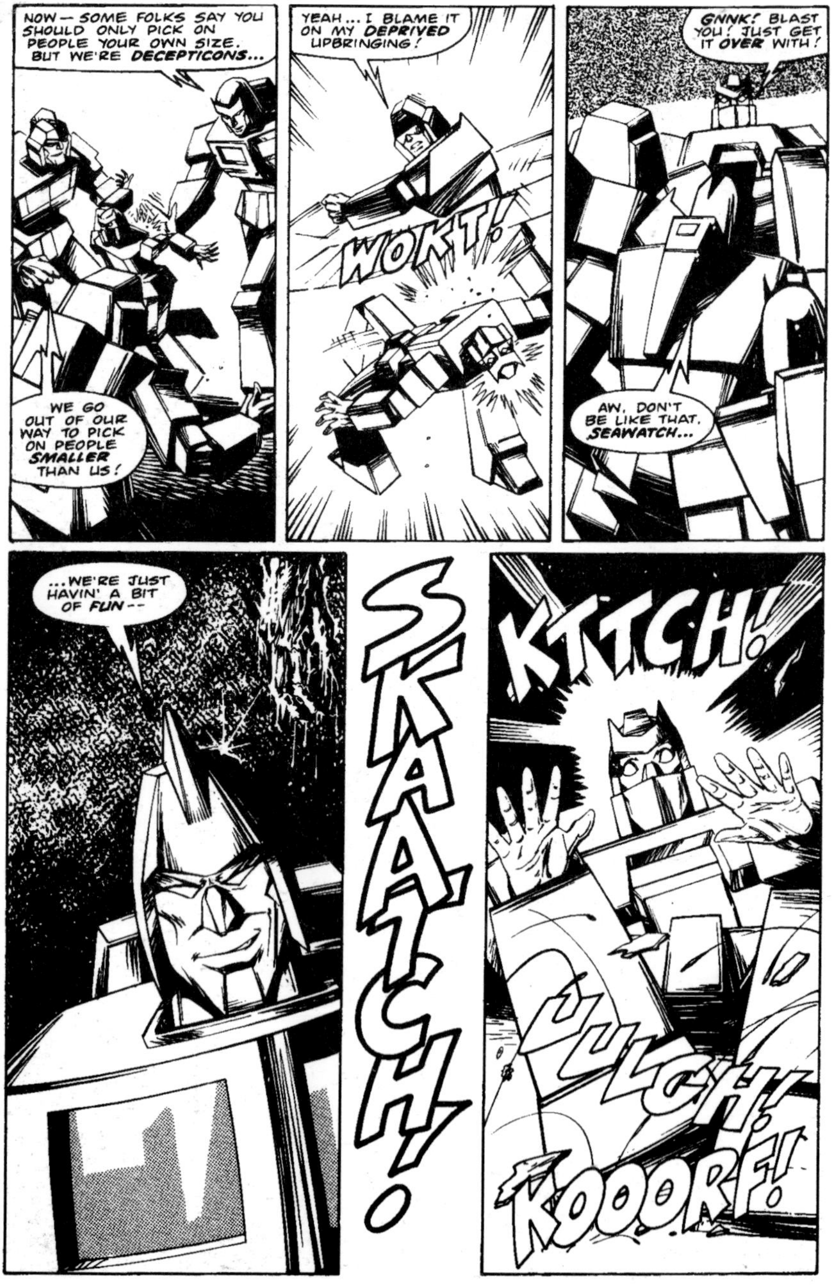

NOW — SOME FOLKS SAY YOU SHOULD ONLY PICK ON PEOPLE YOUR OWN SIZE. BUT WE'RE DECEPTICONS...
WE GO OUT OF OUR WAY TO PICK ON PEOPLE SMALLER THAN US!
YEAH... I BLAME IT ON MY DEPRIVED UPBRINGING!
WOKT!
GNNK! BLAST YOU! JUST GET IT OVER WITH!
AW, DON'T BE LIKE THAT, SEAWATCH...
...WE'RE JUST HAVIN' A BIT OF FUN--
SKAATCH!
KTTCH!
ULLCH!
KOOORF!

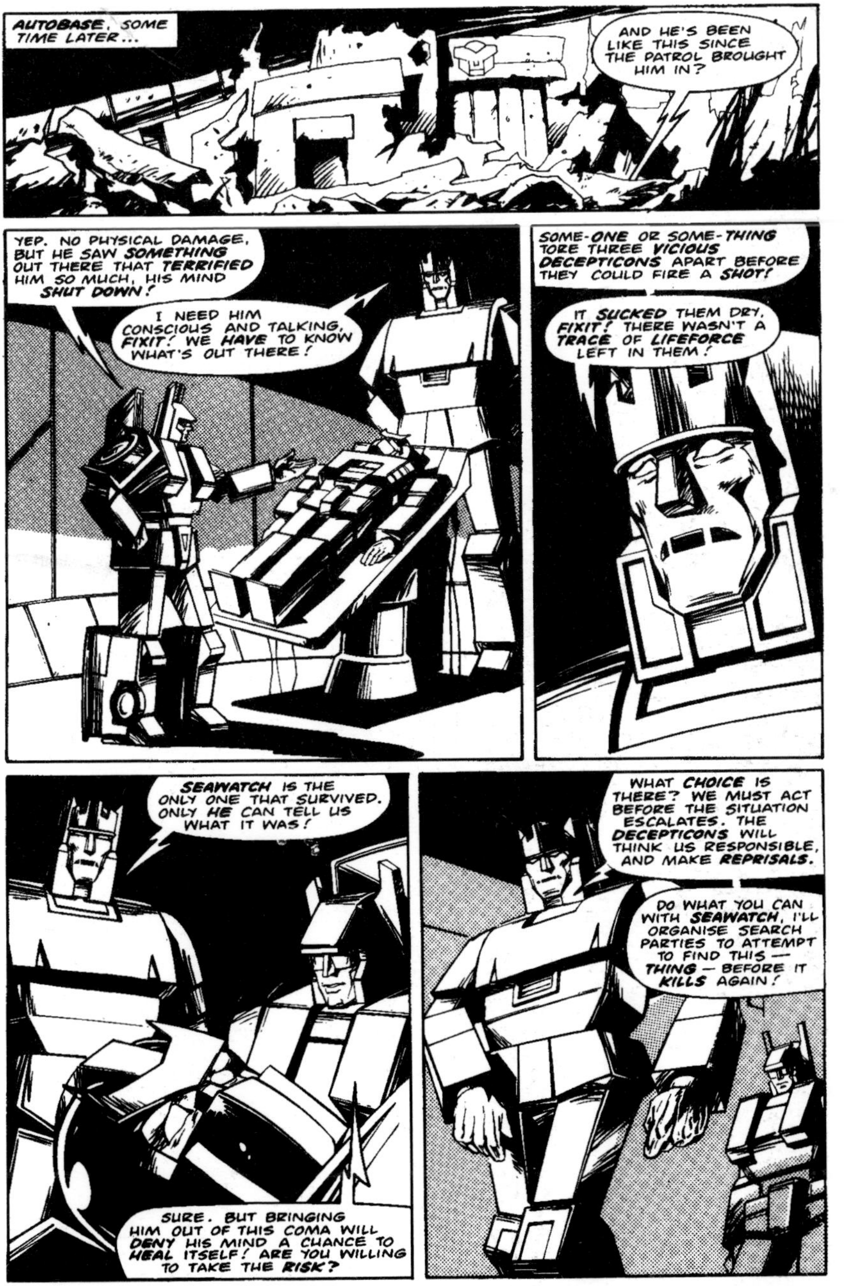
AUTOBASE. SOME TIME LATER...
AND HE'S BEEN LIKE THIS SINCE THE PATROL BROUGHT HIM IN?
YEP. NO PHYSICAL DAMAGE, BUT HE SAW SOMETHING OUT THERE THAT TERRIFIED HIM SO MUCH, HIS MIND SHUT DOWN!
I NEED HIM CONSCIOUS AND TALKING, FIXIT! WE HAVE TO KNOW WHAT'S OUT THERE!
SOME-ONE OR SOME-THING TORE THREE VICIOUS DECEPTICONS APART BEFORE THEY COULD FIRE A SHOT!
IT SUCKED THEM DRY, FIXIT! THERE WASN'T A TRACE OF LIFEFORCE LEFT IN THEM!
SEAWATCH IS THE ONLY ONE THAT SURVIVED. ONLY HE CAN TELL US WHAT IT WAS!
SURE. BUT BRINGING HIM OUT OF THIS COMA WILL DENY HIS MIND A CHANCE TO HEAL ITSELF! ARE YOU WILLING TO TAKE THE RISK?
WHAT CHOICE IS THERE? WE MUST ACT BEFORE THE SITUATION ESCALATES. THE DECEPTICONS WILL THINK US RESPONSIBLE, AND MAKE REPRISALS.
DO WHAT YOU CAN WITH SEAWATCH, I'LL ORGANISE SEARCH PARTIES TO ATTEMPT TO FIND THIS — THING — BEFORE IT KILLS AGAIN!

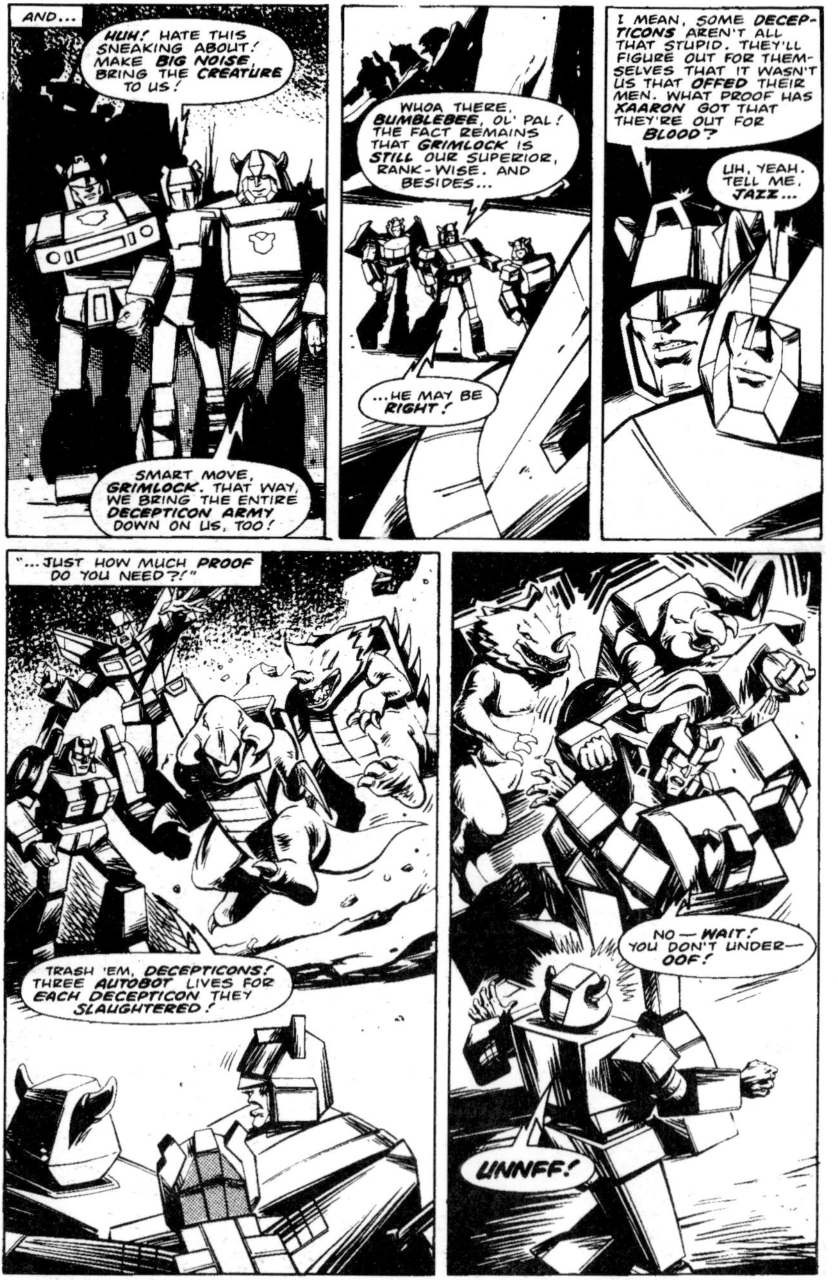
AND...
HUH! HATE THIS SNEAKING ABOUT! MAKE BIG NOISE, BRING THE CREATURE TO US!
SMART MOVE, GRIMLOCK. THAT WAY, WE BRING THE ENTIRE DECEPTICON ARMY DOWN ON US, TOO!
WHOA THERE, BUMBLEBEE, OL' PAL! THE FACT REMAINS THAT GRIMLOCK IS STILL OUR SUPERIOR, RANK-WISE. AND BESIDES...
...HE MAY BE RIGHT!
I MEAN, SOME DECEPTICONS AREN'T ALL THAT STUPID. THEY'LL FIGURE OUT FOR THEMSELVES THAT IT WASN'T US THAT OFFED THEIR MEN. WHAT PROOF HAS XAARON GOT THAT THEY'RE OUT FOR BLOOD?
UH, YEAH. TELL ME, JAZZ...
"...JUST HOW MUCH PROOF DO YOU NEED?!"
TRASH 'EM, DECEPTICONS! THREE AUTOBOT LIVES FOR EACH DECEPTICON THEY SLAUGHTERED!
NO—WAIT! YOU DON'T UNDER— OOF!
UNNFF!

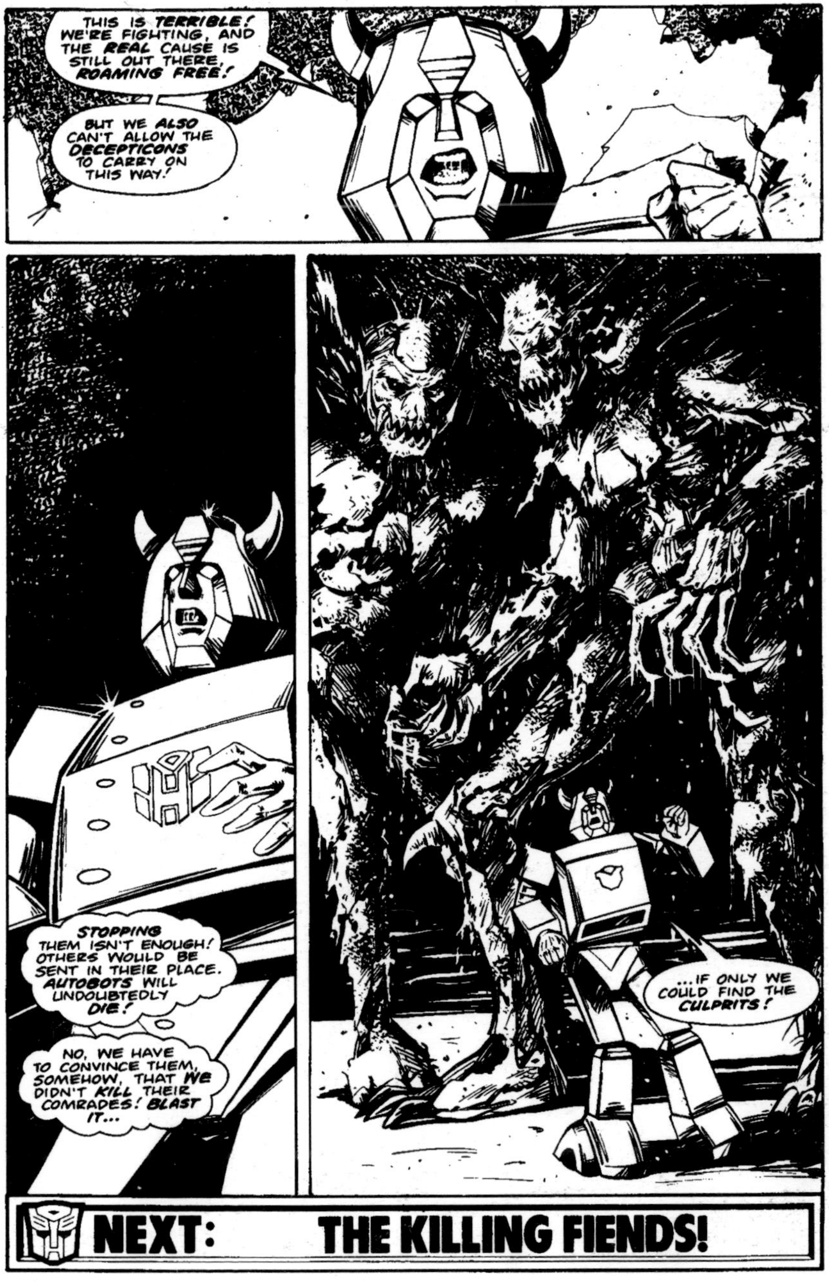
THIS IS TERRIBLE! WE'RE FIGHTING, AND THE REAL CAUSE IS STILL OUT THERE, ROAMING FREE!
BUT WE ALSO CAN'T ALLOW THE DECEPTICONS TO CARRY ON THIS WAY!
STOPPING THEM ISN'T ENOUGH! OTHERS WOULD BE SENT IN THEIR PLACE. AUTOBOTS WILL UNDOUBTEDLY DIE!
NO, WE HAVE TO CONVINCE THEM, SOMEHOW, THAT WE DIDN'T KILL THEIR COMRADES! BLAST IT...
...IF ONLY WE COULD FIND THE CULPRITS!
NEXT: THE KILLING FIENDS!

TRANSFORMERS™

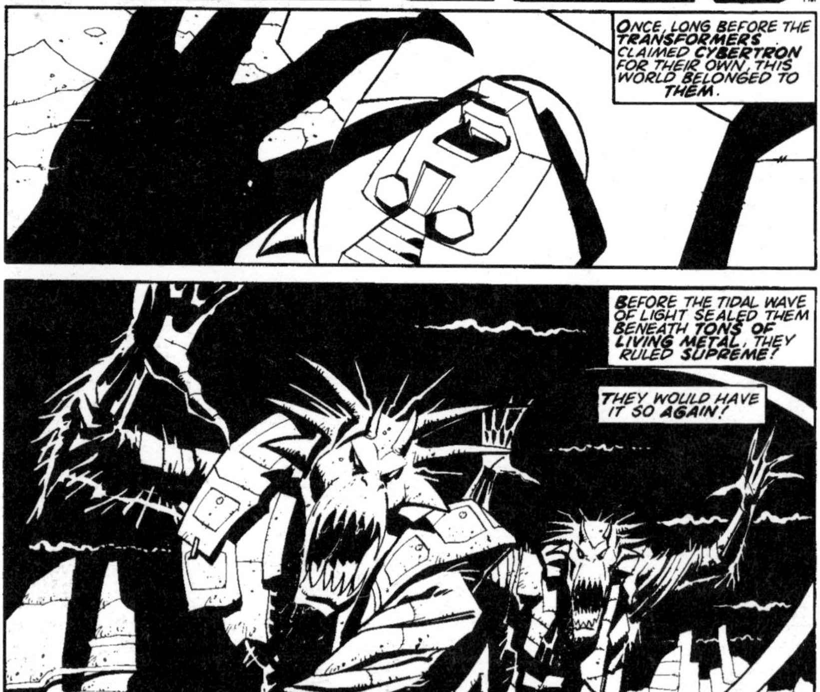
ONCE, LONG BEFORE THE TRANSFORMERS CLAIMED CYBERTRON FOR THEIR OWN, THIS WORLD BELONGED TO THEM.
BEFORE THE TIDAL WAVE OF LIGHT SEALED THEM BENEATH TONS OF LIVING METAL, THEY RULED SUPREME!
THEY WOULD HAVE IT SO AGAIN!
SKREEEK!
MATRIX PRESERVE US!
DAWN OF DARKNESS

Script Simon Furman **Art** Geoff Senior **Letters** Glib

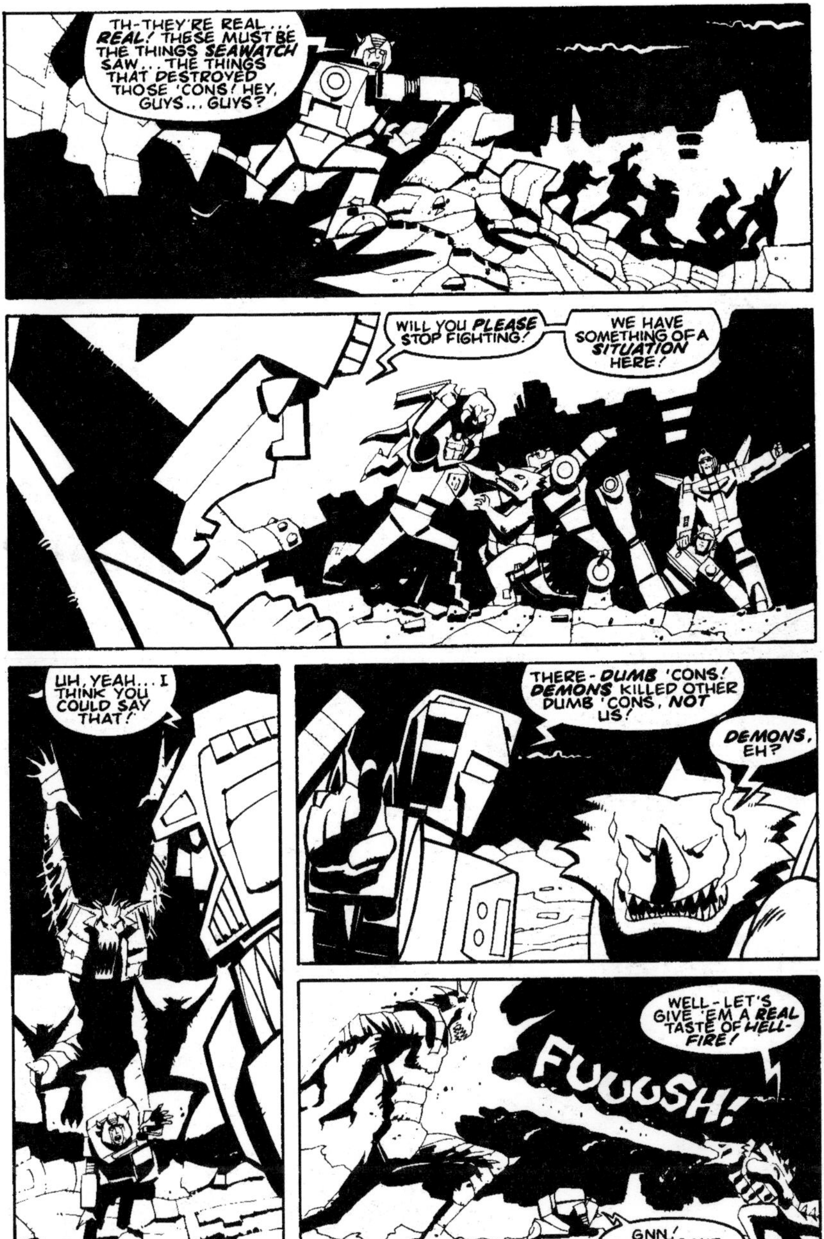
TH-THEY'RE REAL... *REAL!* THESE MUST BE THE THINGS *SEAWATCH* SAW... THE THINGS THAT *DESTROYED* THOSE 'CONS! HEY, GUYS... GUYS?
WILL YOU *PLEASE* STOP FIGHTING!
WE HAVE SOMETHING OF A *SITUATION* HERE!
UH, YEAH... I THINK YOU COULD SAY THAT!
THERE- *DUMB* 'CONS! *DEMONS* KILLED OTHER DUMB 'CONS, *NOT* US!
DEMONS, EH?
WELL-LET'S GIVE 'EM A *REAL* TASTE OF *HELL-FIRE!*
FUUUSH!
GNN! *CINDERSAUR...*

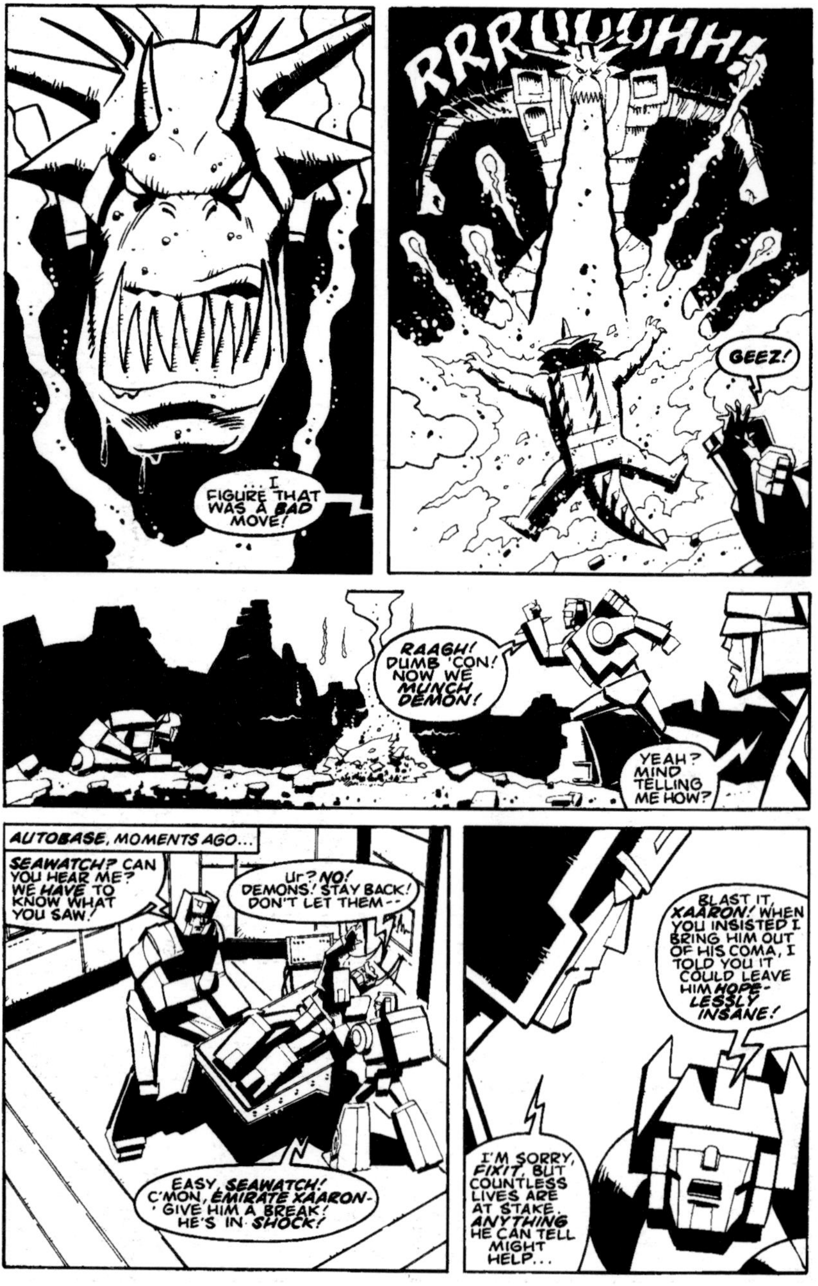
...I FIGURE THAT WAS A BAD MOVE!
RRROOOUHH!
GEEZ!
RAAGH! DUMB 'CON! NOW WE MUNCH DEMON!
YEAH? MIND TELLING ME HOW?
AUTOBASE, MOMENTS AGO...
SEAWATCH? CAN YOU HEAR ME? WE HAVE TO KNOW WHAT YOU SAW!
Ur? NO! DEMONS! STAY BACK! DON'T LET THEM--
EASY, SEAWATCH! C'MON, EMIRATE XAARON - GIVE HIM A BREAK! HE'S IN SHOCK!
BLAST IT, XAARON! WHEN YOU INSISTED I BRING HIM OUT OF HIS COMA, I TOLD YOU IT COULD LEAVE HIM HOPE-LESSLY INSANE!
I'M SORRY, FIXIT, BUT COUNTLESS LIVES ARE AT STAKE. ANYTHING HE CAN TELL MIGHT HELP...

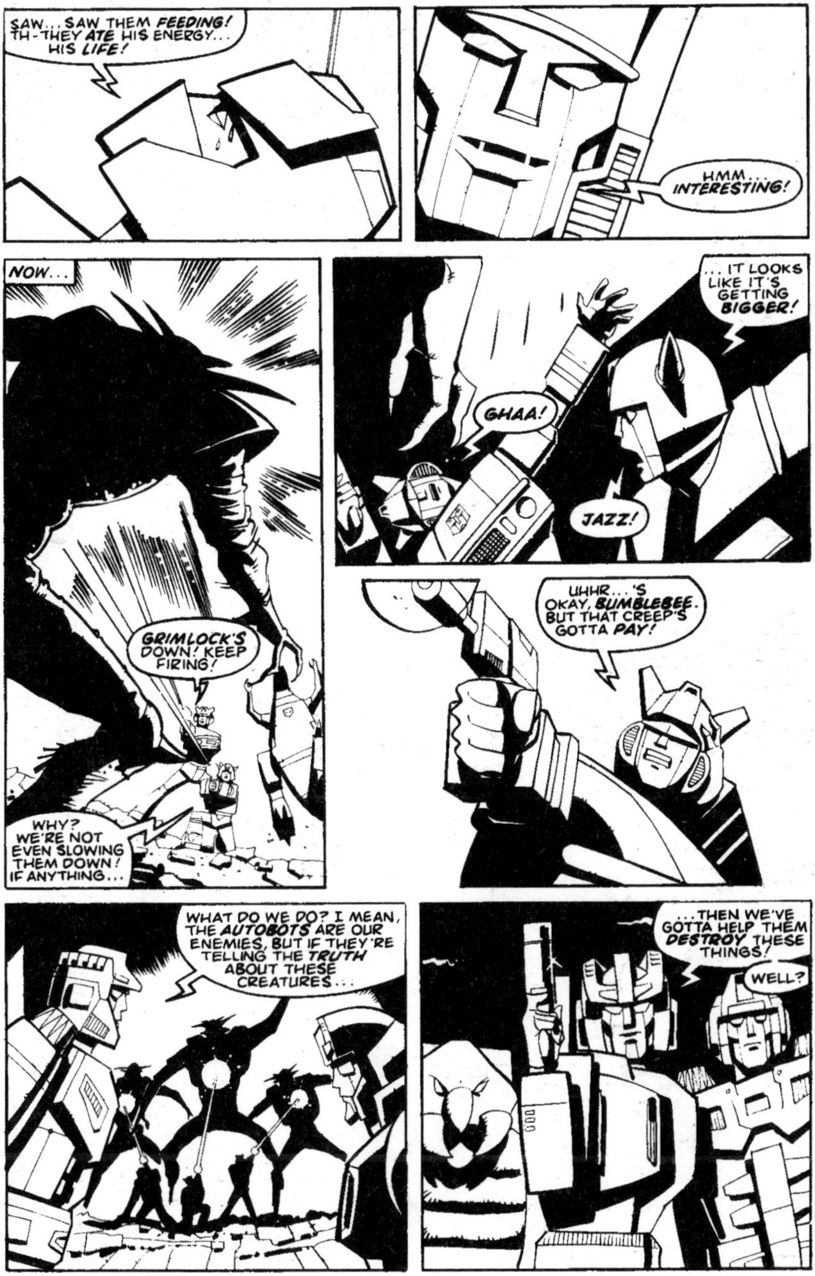
SAW... SAW THEM FEEDING! TH-THEY ATE HIS ENERGY... HIS LIFE!
HMM... INTERESTING!
NOW...
GRIMLOCK'S DOWN! KEEP FIRING!
WHY? WE'RE NOT EVEN SLOWING THEM DOWN! IF ANYTHING...
... IT LOOKS LIKE IT'S GETTING BIGGER!
GHAA!
JAZZ!
UHHR...'S OKAY, BUMBLEBEE. BUT THAT CREEP'S GOTTA PAY!
WHAT DO WE DO? I MEAN, THE AUTOBOTS ARE OUR ENEMIES, BUT IF THEY'RE TELLING THE TRUTH ABOUT THESE CREATURES...
...THEN WE'VE GOTTA HELP THEM DESTROY THESE THINGS!
WELL?

THE BATTLE IS JOINED IN EARNEST, BUT IT SOON BECOMES APPARENT...

IT'S NOT WORKING! THEY'RE ABSORBING OUR ENERGY BEAMS - FEEDING OFF THEM!

INDEED. AND IF WHAT I BELIEVE IS TRUE, TO CONTINUE TO DO SO IS THE ONLY WAY OF STOPPING THEM!

XAARON? WHAT'S GOING ON?

NOW, RED HOT!

THAT'S PURE ENERGON I'M FEEDING THEM! ACCORDING TO LEGEND, THESE CREATURES FEED ON OTHERS' LIFEFORCE ... THEIR ENERGY!

I'M GAMBLING THAT THEIR SYSTEMS CAN ONLY TOLERATE SO MUCH INTAKE AT ONCE BEFORE--

SHREEE!

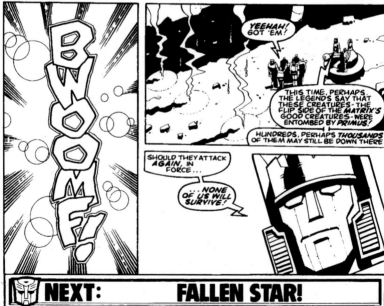

BWOOMF!

YEEHAH! GOT 'EM!

THIS TIME, PERHAPS. THE LEGENDS SAY THAT THESE CREATURES - THE FLIP SIDE OF THE MATRIX'S GOOD CREATURES - WERE ENTOMBED BY PRIMUS!

HUNDREDS, PERHAPS THOUSANDS OF THEM MAY STILL BE DOWN THERE.

SHOULD THEY ATTACK AGAIN, IN FORCE...

...NONE OF US WILL SURVIVE!

NEXT: FALLEN STAR!

Writer — Simon Furman
Artists — Jeff Anderson, Simon Coleby, Staz Johnson
Geoff Senior, Art Wetherall & Andrew Wildman
Inkers — Simon Coleby & Tim Perkins
Letterers — Helen Stone & Gary Gilbert
Original series editor — Euan Peters

Simon Furman began his long relationship with *Transformers* with issue #13 of the UK comic. Since then, Furman's comics work has included *Transformers* (US), *Transformers: Generation 2*, *Death's Head*, *Alpha Flight* and *Turok*. Furman has also scripted episodes for animated TV series such as *Beast Wars*, *Dan Dare* and *X-Men: Evolution*. His most recent work includes *Transformers: Energon* and *The War Within* and he is the author of Dorling Kindersley's *Transformers: The Ultimate Guide*.

Andrew Wildman's artwork has featured in *X-Men Adventures*, *GI Joe* and *Spider-Man 2099*. He is currently drawing online comic *The Engine* and designing characters for TV animation.

Stuart 'Staz' Johnson has had success with his *Batman/Aliens 2* crossover and has also done sterling work on both *Catwoman* and *Robin*.

Simon Coleby has worked largely for the UK comics industry with his work appearing in *Transformers*, *Death's Head* and *2000 AD*. He also worked on *Punisher 2099* for Marvel US.

Geoff Senior is a UK based artist who has worked on many titles during the '80s including *Transformers*, *2000 AD*, *Dragon's Claws*, *Death's Head* and *What If?*

COMING soon...

Transformers is a trademark of Hasbro.
© 2005 Hasbro. All Rights Reserved.

DISCARDED

TRANSFORMERS
WAY OF THE WARRIOR

ISBN: 1 84576 059 X
Collects Transformers:
UK black and white material from issues
#219-222, 229, 237-239, 272-274,
282, 283 & 249-250.

DEC 1 4 2007